The Folklore of the British Isles
General Editor: Venetia J. Newall

The Folklore
of the
Scottish Highlands

'For Berenice'

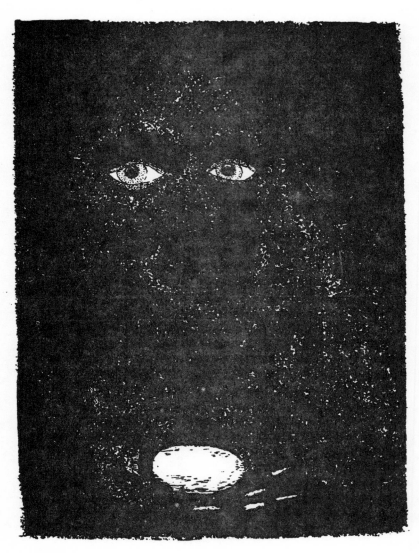

Brahan Seer

The Folklore
of the
Scottish Highlands

ANNE ROSS
Drawings by Richard Feachem

BARNES
&NOBLE
B O O K S
NEW YORK

This edition published by Barnes & Noble, Inc.,
by arrangement with B. T. Batsford Ltd.

1993 Barnes & Noble Books

ISBN 1-56619-226-9

Printed and bound in the United States of America

M 9 8 7 6 5

Contents

Acknowledgments

It is not possible to express adequately here my deep affection for the people of the Highlands and Islands of Scotland and the delight that their unique heritage of folklore and folksong never fail to bring to me. I would wish to record my sincere gratitude to the numerous Gaels who, at home in the Highlands, or in exile elsewhere, have given up hours of their precious time in conversation about the old traditions and superstitions, and have patiently and generously recited tales and legends, poetry and song which reached them through many generations of their ancestry. Their hospitality is unrivalled and their company without equal. It is not possible to name them all, and to select a few would imply that others, equally deserving of thanks, have been forgotten. I would however like to pay tribute to the people of North Uist, and especially the Ferguson family at Carinish who, as a school-girl, took me into their home and taught me their language with infinite patience and kindness. They also introduced me to the charmed life of the island and its people in a way which would otherwise have been quite impossible. I must also acknowledge with humility and gratitude the work of all the great collectors of the past who battled heroically to salvage as much of the still-rich tradition as they could, without the aids with which present-day field-workers are equipped. Today, the dedicated work of the School of Scottish Studies in the University of Edinburgh carries on the valiant work of recording and preserving as much of the rapidly-dying tradition as it can. Many friends have helped me in a variety of ways, especially John and Marjorie Exall, both spiritually, and by providing me with a place of peace and quiet in which to work. I am indebted to the Folklore Society for the provision of essential books, to the publishers for kind and sympathetic cooperation throughout and to Oliver and Boyd for permission to quote from Alexander Carmichael's *Ortha nan Gaidheal*, Carmina Gadelica (1928-54). The illustration on page 92 is after Shaw, M.F., 1955, 31.

Anne Ross

Foreword

In 1871 Queen Victoria's daughter, Princess Louise, married John Douglas Sutherland Campbell, heir to the 8th Duke of Argyll, and 'Wasna' the Queen a proud woman!', commented *Punch*. The wedding underlines the important historical role of the Highlands. As Argyllshire's Director of Education, Colin MacDonald, points out: '. . . the prominence of the 9 Campbell Earls of Argyll in Scottish history and of the subsequent 11 Dukes of Argyll in the history of Great Britain is unsurpassed by any other single noble British family.'

Some may question this judgement in detail, but few would reject it out-of-hand. It is especially generous coming from a MacDonald. In 1493, James IV deposed John, last of that name to be Lord of the Isles, and it was on the wreck of the great Clan MacDonald that the Campbells arose. They were to become the most numerous and powerful of all the Highland Clans and, inevitably, the most deeply involved in contention. When the Marquess of Montrose rallied the clans on the King's behalf in 1644, his success derived from hatred of the Campbells, rather than devotion to him or loyalty to the Stewart cause.

Montrose made his final abortive stand for Charles II at Carbisdale in 1650, after marching south through Caithness. Here, thirty years later, the Campbells overcame the Sinclairs in the last major clan battle. Their triumph in 1650 led to the execution of Montrose in Edinburgh on 21 May, though eleven years and six days later his great opponent, the first Marquess of Argyll, was to follow him to the scaffold. It is endearing to find a socialist stalwart like Karl Marx giving approval to Argyll, because he was beheaded by royalists. Marx supposed, incorrectly, that the Marquess was an ancestor of his wife. True, Mrs. Marx was a quarter Scots, but her Scottish grandmother's name, Jane Wishart, leads back to Sir John Wishart of Pitarrow, near Montrose. It was in the Montrose domain that Sir John died in 1607 — his grandfather was half-cousin to George Wishart, the Protestant martyr.

But Marx was in fact connected with the Argylls. In 1881, a few days after his wife's death, he explained to his daughter, Jenny, that Mrs. Marx' grandfather had married a close relative of the Argylls. . . . One does not need to be informed on such matters except that, if one is not, one cannot set oneself up to correct other "biographers".' Jenny must have been amused, had it occurred to her that she was a distant cousin of Queen Victoria's son-in-law: the husband of Princess Louise and 9th Duke-to-be was at that time Governor General of Canada. This relationship also links the Marx family to a pioneer Scottish folklorist.

Jane Wishart was granddaughter of John Campbell of Orchard, a descendant of the 2nd Earl of Argyll, though not of the Marquess. From 1727, John Campbell was Duke's factor of Kintyre, a MacDonald territory which fell to the Campbells scarcely more than a century earlier. Islay, off Kintyre to the west, had long been the headquarters of the Lords of the Isles and their MacDonald descendants. Here, in James VI's reign, they were attacked by the MacLeans of Mull, who had won the king's sympathy. The invasion was unsuccessful but, as a result, Islay and Kintyre were granted to the Campbells. All now left to the MacDonalds of their ancestors' great island kingdom was the islet of Cara and a nearby property on Kintyre. Indeed, with the title annexed to the crown since 1540, the Lordship, which once stretched from Lewis to the Isle of Man, and included large areas of the mainland, was scarcely more than a memory.

Their forebears repeatedly sacked Iona, the Athos of Celtic Christianity, and yet it was the Lords of the Isles who re-established it in 1203. The Cathedral's modern history dates from the late nineteenth century, when their Campbell successors presented it to the Church of Scotland. This was thanks to the 8th Duke of Argyll, Princess Louise's father-in-law and titular successor to John Campbell of Orchard's employer. He combined ardent respect for the past with a genuine interest in current scientific theory — particularly in its reconciliation with Christian belief. His cousin, and exact contemporary, was John Campbell of Islay (1822-85), whose work as a folktale collector owes much to the Duke's friendship and encouragement. Though sometimes marred by the fanciful ideas fashionable at the time, Campbell was, for his day, a remarkably methodical worker. Perhaps the Duke's scientific notions were an influence, as well as, more demonstrably, the linguistic researches of the Brothers Grimm. The Grimms were to nineteenth-century linguistics what Marx was to contemporary radical politics, so here is an intellectual link far closer than the distant family relationship.

It was the Grimms' folktale studies which particular attracted John Campbell, and the advice he received from his friend, George Dasent, places him, of all the early British folklorists, most directly in their tradition. Dasent, later Assistant Editor of *The Times,* much admired the Grimms' ideology, and actually met Jacob in 1840.

Anne Ross published her wonderful book, *Pagan Celtic Britain,* 107 years after Campbell brought out his still invaluable *Popular Tales of the West Highlands.* Her comment on previous scholars in her own field is worth noting, especially compared with the emphasis preferred by Campbell and his generation: '. . . the material is inflected to suit whatever particular theory they are advancing and modern folklore becomes inextricably confused with the early literary traditions . . . archaeology . . . is largely ignored except where it can supposedly be used to support an already firmly held theory.' Anne Ross, and others of similar outlook, deserve our praise; by recognising that folklore studies must be truly catholic, they have helped to make the discipline increasingly relevant. Her contribution to this series is most welcome: it will delight not only serious folklorists, but those with a more general interest and, of course, all lovers of Scotland.

Venetia Newall

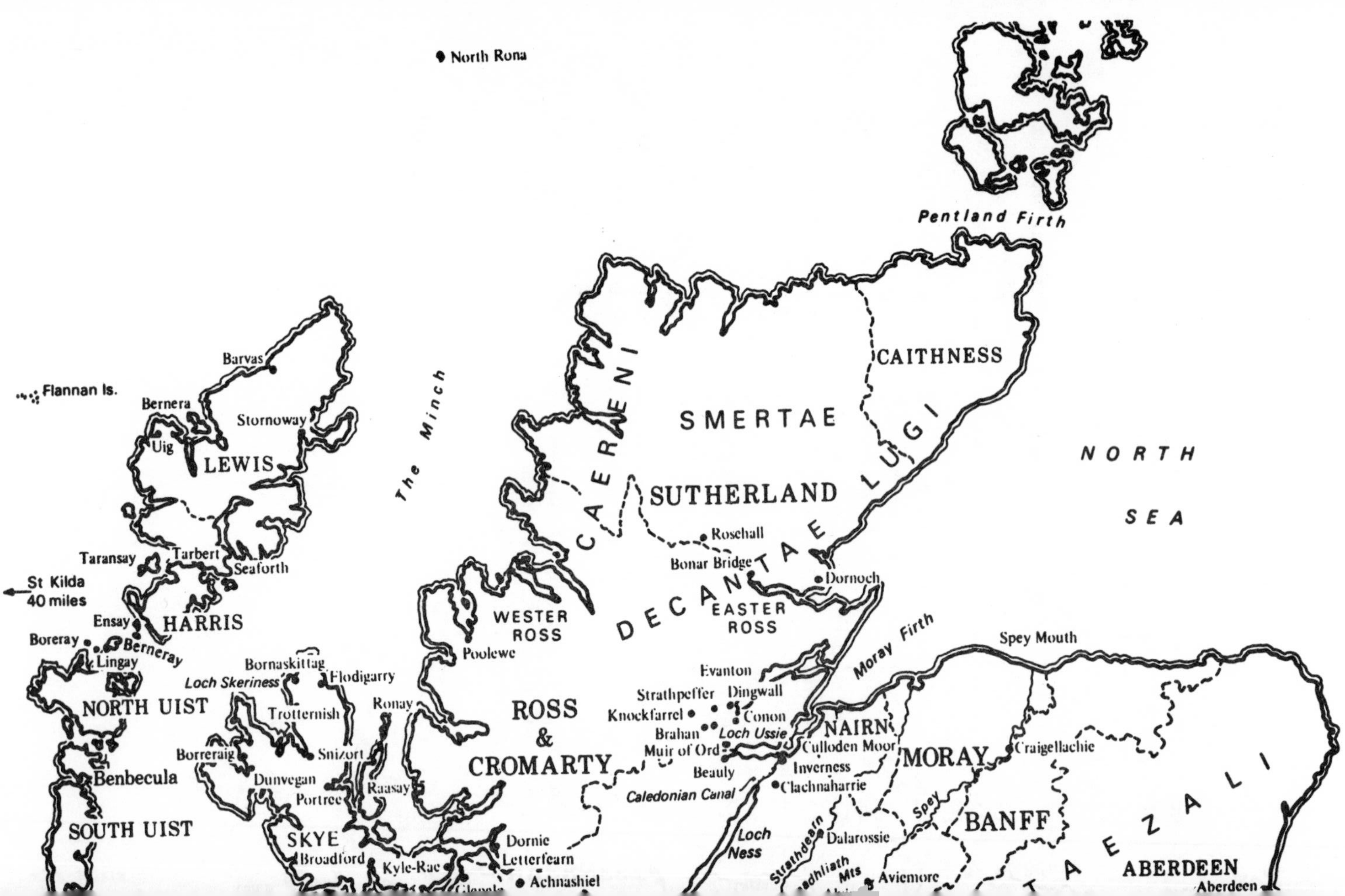
North Rona
Pentland Firth
Flannan Is.
Barvas
Bernera
Stornoway
Uig
LEWIS
The Minch
CAERENI
SMERTAE
CAITHNESS
LUGI
NORTH
SEA
SUTHERLAND
Rosehall
Bonar Bridge
DECANTAE
Dornoch
Taransay
Tarbert
Seaforth
St Kilda
40 miles
Ensay
HARRIS
Boreray
Berneray
Lingay
WESTER
ROSS
EASTER
ROSS
Poolewe
Moray Firth
Spey Mouth
Evanton
Bornaskittag
Flodigarry
Loch Skeriness
NORTH UIST
Trotternish
Ronay
ROSS
&
CROMARTY
Strathpeffer
Dingwall
Knockfarrel
Conon
Brahan
Loch Ussie
NAIRN
Muir of Ord
Culloden Moor
MORAY
Craigellachie
Borreraig
Snizort
Benbecula
Dunvegan
Raasay
Beauly
Inverness
Caledonian Canal
Clachnaharrie
Portree
SOUTH UIST
SKYE
Broadford
Kyle-Rae
Dornie
Letterfearn
Achnashiel
Loch
Ness
Strathdearn
Dalarossie
Spey
BANFF
TAEZALI
Mts
Aviemore
ABERDEEN
Aberdeen

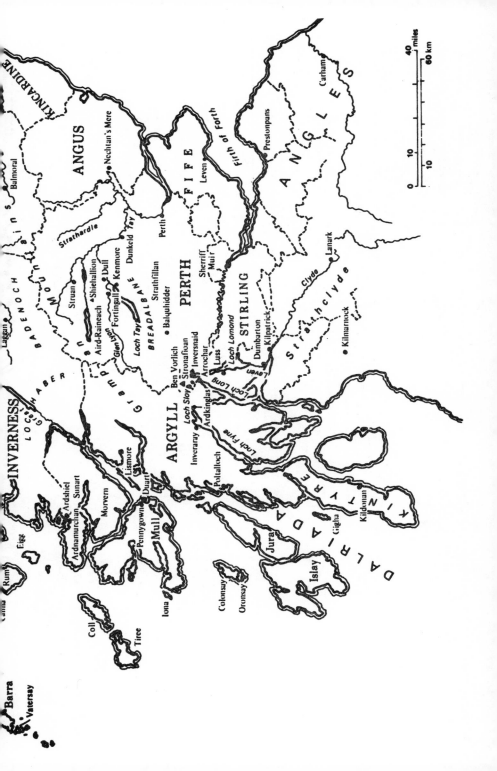

Caereni

Lugi

Smertae

Picts

Decantea

Taezali

Picts

Picts

Caledonii

Schiehallion ⊕

Dunkeld

Dalriada

ANTONINE
WALL

Scots

Angles

Strathclyde
Britons

Dalriada

HADRIAN'S WALL

0   50 Miles

Foot waulking

—◁ 1 ▷—

Introduction

Two boys, whose birth beyond all question springs
From great and glorious, tho' forgotten kings,
Shepherds of *Scottish* lineage, born and bred
On the same bleak and barren mountain's head,
Jockey with mickle art, could on the bagpipes play,
E'en from the rising to the setting day;
Sawney as long without remorse could bawl
HOME 's madrigals and ditties from FINGAL.

IN THESE lines from his *Prophecy of Famine,* the strongly
anti-Scottish priest-poet, Charles Churchill, writing from his living
under the shadow of another Celtic stronghold, South Cadbury in
Somerset, showed a subtle knowledge and appreciation of an
ancient tradition, the rich heritage of Gaelic Scotland. In his day
Highland folklore, story and superstition were still very much in
evidence. And in the somewhat scathing lines above, Churchill has
noted subtleties of that archaic culture which are still discernible,

11

albeit it in aetiolated form, down to the present day. The Celtic predilection for ancestry and belief in the ultimate nobility of their forefathers (forgotten though these regal forebears may now be except to those who immortalise them in the recitation of their *sloinneadh*, 'naming of ancestors'); pride in their Scottish nationality; cultivating the ancient arts of their country in physical discomfort and humble circumstances; the tireless playing of the bagpipes, their musical variety of pattern as ingenious and as amazingly varied as the designs their forebears wrought with infinite skill upon the metal and the wood and the pottery of the past; the ancient chanted tales of the Fingalian heroes, still to be heard in the glens and islands of the west; all these fundamental aspects of the tradition were observed, if not approved, by the great English writer.

As in ancient pagan times, when the classical writers were commenting on the customs and habits of their Celtic neighbours in Europe and Britain, and the splendid repertoire of Irish and British legend and myth was receiving written form by the early Christian scribes, the life of the Scottish Highlander was, up to comparatively recent times, not only rich in lore and legend, music and song, but completely hedged round by tabu – things to be done, things to be avoided. The whole of everyday life was circumscribed by the powers, good and evil, that were believed to be everywhere present, to be placated by ritual or exploited by magical processes. The otherworld forces, and the ghosts and monsters of hill and water were as real, substantial, and infinitely more menacing than one's own neighbours. Every place had its name and its legend – how it got its name; what famous hero or infamous criminal, savage, supernatural animal, or shaggy, semi-human sprite was associated with it were stories known at one time to all. This Celtic predilection for immediate locality, the love and knowledge of not only the homeland, but every detail of the native landscape, is an absolutely fundamental characteristic of the Celts, linked with their ancient and passionate love of nature and their feeling for the world of birds and animals which manifests itself so early in their recorded history. Ancient tales about the gods and goddesses, and heroes long dead and gone are still told with simple sincerity and total credulity by those in whom the tradition still lives and who, like the ancient Celtic god, Ogmios, holds the ears of his listeners enchained to the eloquence and fluency of his native tongue. The tendency was – and to a vestigial extent is – for each community to have its *seanachaidh*, 'tale-teller', par excellence. The Highlanders have always loved stories and a whole group from a township would gather together in the *tigh-chéilidh*, or house of entertainment, to pass the long, dark and often wild winter nights listening enraptured to tales, many of incredible length, some of almost unbelievable antiquity, which formed part of the rich store of oral tradition, which itself is commented upon as early as the writings of Caesar. These stories were handed on by word of mouth, from generation to generation, the archaic nuclei gathering to themselves new elements from a wealth of external sources, taking material from international folklore and folktale motifs, and blending it skilfully with the old, indigenous elements. Over and above the story-tellers – who tended on the whole to be men in the west of Scotland – there were those who could chant the ancient ballads, many of which contain legends common to Ireland and Scotland, and can still be recorded today, although the rich heritage of such material is dying fast. There were also the experts on the proverbial sayings, of which hundreds must have circulated at one time in the remote Celtic world; and those with powers, good and evil – people who were believed to be able to practice witchcraft and woe, and others who were known as 'white' witches, the charmers and healers who could undo the spells of malice and replace them by healing and protection. Then there were the singers of songs, much loved by the whole community. At one time, communal labour, or individual chores, were accompanied by, and made less burdensome by songs, and the repertoire of these is one of the richest features of the Gaelic folk tradition. There were rowing songs, reaping songs, milking songs, churning songs; songs to soothe the tired infant, songs to lighten the heavy task of querning the grain. But the richest and most important group of songs in the entire tradition are those known as *òrain luadhaidh* or 'waulking' songs, songs sung to facilitate the heavy labour of 'waulking' or shrinking by hand the tweed and make the sturdy Highland cloth proof against rough country and wet, inclement weather. Many of these are still extant, for the communal occupation of waulking did not die out until the present century when the electric looms and factory facilities rendered redundant the old, heavy, but happy work of the strong, competent hands of the

Hebridean women. In the waulking songs are preserved some of the most ancient historical and mythological material — ballads, fairy songs, clan lore, songs of love and stories of heroism; fights against monsters, human and supernatural; and witty local anecdotes, some with a naughty dig against the men, or a particular local character. In these songs alone lurks a wealth of information on the traditional life of the Highlands and its ancient tales and customs.

The waulking songs themselves are of profound interest and are unparalleled elsewhere in the west of Europe. The whole process of the communal shrinking of the handwoven cloth, thus preparing it for the tailor's shears, is fascinating. It was — and remained — an occupation reserved for the womenfolk and the men were firmly excluded from the activity. Originally the women sat on the ground and pounded the cloth on a wooden trestle with their feet; later the hands alone were used for this purpose, the women sitting, or standing on either side of a table. The astonishing impact of this unfamiliar ritual on a stranger to the west is well expressed by Martin Martin, in his description of North Uist. He describes how a party of people from an English ship landed on the island and one of them came upon a house in which were ten women, behaving, to the Englishman, in an extremely strange manner. Their arms and legs were bare and they were sitting, five on either side of a board which was placed between them; on this was a length of cloth which they were thickening with their hands and feet, and singing the whole time. 'The Englishman presently concluded it to be a little Bedlam, which they did not expect to find in so remote a corner.' The episode was recounted to the owner of the island, a Mr John MacLean, who said he had never seen any mad people in the islands. This did not convince, so the leader of the party and the proprietor went to the house where the women were working. Mr MacLean then told the stranger that this was merely the common way of thickening the cloth in those parts; the Englishman had to accept the information but remained astonished at the scene he had witnessed.

The wool from which the tweed was woven was first dyed to the desired colour in a dye made from vegetable matter of various kinds. When it was ready, the loom was set, and, as with most important everyday activities, there were lucky and unlucky days for this — another archaic Celtic belief. One of these, in the Island of South

Uist was St Columba's Day – 9 June – perhaps the most beloved of the saints in the Catholic Highlands:

> Thursday the day of kindly Columba,
> The day to gather the sheep in the fold,
> To set the loom, and put cows with the calves.

When the cloth is woven it is soaked in a vat of hot, stale urine, which has been collected for the purpose for some time. The ends of the length of cloth are then sewn together to make a complete circle which is next placed on a trestle table, or even the door of the byre if nothing better is available and about a dozen women sit at the table, an even number on either side, and pass the heavy cloth to each other, sunwise (to the left), kneading it vigorously in four decisive rhythmic movements. As they work they sing, the leader telling the story of the song and the others chanting the refrain. It is a fascinating scene to witness, the heaviness of the labour lightened by the enjoyment of the singing, and the whole vast repertoire of songs enshrining and preserving some of the most rare and ancient aspects of the folk tradition. Songs originally used for other communal activities, which have become redundant, often found their way into the stock of waulking songs; thus, over and above its importance for the anthropologist and the musicologist, the practice of waulking the cloth to the accompaniment of song is one of first interest and value to the folklorist.

The Highlands and Islands of the west contain both Protestant and Catholic communities. In the Outer Hebrides North Uist and the islands to the north are Protestant, part of Benbecula and all the southern isles Catholic. Like the old Celtic Church in Ireland, the Catholic priests have a greater tolerance for the old customs which were at one time feared and disliked by the Protestant ministers as being representative of pagan decadence. As a result, the extant traditions in the Catholic areas differ from those of the Protestant regions, being, in many ways, more archaic and rich; but the Protestant areas retained much of their lore and have their own valuable contribution to make to an understanding of tale, custom and belief which, even today, is so astonishingly rich and varied in the Scottish Highlands.

Calendar festivals have always been closely observed by the Celts and in these, much that is purely pagan has survived, blended often almost inextricably with Christian feasts. Festivities connected, for example, with the ancient pan-Celtic god Lugus (Lugh), which we know to have taken place in Gaul on 1 August at the time of Caesar's wars there, survived vestigially all over the Celtic world down to the present century and have been the subject of a recent fascinating study. The feast, which took place on, or near 1 August and was known as *Lughnasa*, 'the feast in honour of Lugh's birth', was not a harvest thanksgiving, but a feast of propitiation – a blessing of the harvest to be reaped. The festivities took place frequently on some hill or eminence; there was often a 'patten' – a procession – round some sacred well, led by the priest; games, markets, races and communal activity of every kind ensued. At the various calendar festivals in the Protestant areas the Trinity was invoked; in the Catholic regions pagan deities metamorphosed into local saints were added to the Trinity and the more common orthodox saints, and in the southern Outer Hebrides Saint Michael was on occasion invoked as the god Michael. Hallowe'en, the ancient feast of *Samhuin,* the night before 1 November, continued to be regarded as the most awesome period of the year, a time when the powers of the Otherworld became visible – and often dangerous – to mankind, and when human sacrifice and propitiation were essential according to the belief of the pagan Celts, to make benign and satisfy the dark forces of the unknown.

Many of the ancient beliefs and superstitions can still be glimpsed in the treasure-house of the surviving oral tradition, their power gone, their continuity due entirely to the force of the strong folk memory and the longevity of the traditions from which they originally sprang. Stories of the rebellion of 1745 and the evictions of the following decades are related as if they had happened yesterday. Belief in the power of Second Sight is more or less universally present; and the association of prehistoric monuments with past battles fought by gigantic foes is equally widespread. There are still people living in the Gaelic west who claim to have had direct experience of the fairies, and others who assert that they *did* exist until comparatively recently but, like the great shoals of herring that populated the shores of the Hebrides, have now, for some mysterious reason, gone.

It is due to the devoted, tireless and often hazardous work of the great collectors of Gaelic folklore that we have a repertoire of recorded tradition of great size and variety, one which provides a yardstick against which to measure the considerable, but now infinitely more fragmented body of lore still current in the west today. The persecution of the Gaelic language and all that it stood for began long ago. As early as 1567 John Carswell, Bishop of the Isles, wrote: 'Great is the blindness and darkness of sin and ignorance and of understanding among composers and writers and supporters of the Gaelic in that they prefer and practise the framing of vain, hurtful, lying, earthly stories about the *Tuatha De Danann* and about the sons of Milesius and about the heroes and Fionn MacCumhail and his giants and about many others whom I shall not number or tell of here in detail, in order to maintain and advance these, with a view to obtaining for themselves passing worldly gain, rather than to write and to compose and to support the faithful words of God and the perfect way of truth.' In this castigation of the oral tradition, Bishop Carswell gives us valuable information, not only about the vigour with which it was practised, but the nature of its contents. The Tuatha De Danann were the pagan gods of ancient Ireland, known to us through the stories of their deeds, written down by the scribes of the early Christian Church. They were clearly still popular with the people in the sixteenth century; and even today fragmentary stories of their heroic and magical deeds can still be found in remote corners of Gaelic Scotland. The stories of the sons of Mil likewise belong to the early Irish Book of Invasions, that great corpus of semi-historical, semi-mythological material accounting for the coming of the different races – some of them deities – to Ireland. Hero tales, about characters ancient and modern were, and perhaps still are, the most popular of all the long stories; and amongst these rank the stories telling of the fabulous deeds of the semi-supernatural Irish hero, Fionn MacCumhail and his giants, as Carswell calls them, the characters who played the leading role in MacPherson's *Ossian* (Fionn's son by a woman in the form of a hind) which led to the great Ossianic controversy in the eighteenth century and the subsequent focusing of attention of the whole of literary Europe on the Gaelic west. All these subjects are treated in greater detail in the relevant sections of the book.

In spite of persecution by the Protestant Church and by the

education authorities, the Gaelic language and some of its great heritage of oral tradition has survived. Ancient customs and beliefs were commented on, inadvertently as it were, by travellers to the Highlands such as Edward Lhuyd, the Welsh geologist and Celtic linguist, the first collector of Gaelic folklore and compiler of the first Gaelic dictionary in the late seventeenth century; natives like Martin Martin, protestant minister in the Island of Skye, visited the Outer Hebrides a few years later and recorded much valuable material. Again, strangers such as Dr Johnson, making his famous tour of Scotland with the Lowland lawyer, James Boswell in 1773, stimulated by the writings of such as Martin, whose original Description appeared as early as 1703, have valuable fragments to add to the testimony of the surviving oral tradition and the comments of native writers.

The systematic work of collecting extant popular lore in the Scottish Highlands really began in the last century with the great work of John Francis Campbell of Islay (*Iain Òg Ìle,* 'Young John of Islay'). A gentleman by birth, and living at a time when the Gaelic language was despised as being the speech of peasants and the poor, he learnt to speak the native tongue of his island and dedicated himself to travelling far and wide, laboriously writing down every fragment he could find of the once rich folklore. He worked in every kind of condition and left to posterity a unique corpus of material which would otherwise have soon perished under the strong pressures operating against it. In his edition of the Dewar Manuscripts, the Rev. John MacKechnie says of Campbell:

> The collecting of folklore was but one of J. F. Campbell's many activities. He it was who had seen the need of gathering the material and who set up the machinery for doing that; but it was not so much what he actually collected that is important, but rather the example he set before others and the inspiration which fired all who came into contact with him. At a time when Gaelic was neglected and regarded as unworthy of a gentleman's attention, he pointed out its charm and the inestimable value of much that was enshrined in the Gaelic language. He showed that a gentleman might well be proud of his knowledge of Gaelic.

The nature of the great collector, the first of many eminent scholars in this field, is well illustrated by his own comments on his work:

> My wish has been simply to gather some specimens of the wreck so plentifully strewn on the coasts of old Scotland, and to carry it where others may examine it; rather to point out where curious objects worth some attention may be found, rather than to gather a great heap. I have not sought for stranded forests. I have not polished the rough sticks which I found; I have but cut off a very few offending splinters, and I trust that some may be found who will not utterly despise such rubbish, or scorn the magic which peasants attribute to a fairy egg.

John Campbell was primarily interested in the tales told in the Highlands, and these he classified into various types. Another important contemporary collector was Alexander Carmichael who was mainly concerned with the charms and incantations current at the time, although he recorded every piece of Gaelic lore which it was in his power to do. Other distinguished collectors added to the growing body of oral material; today, the School of Scottish Studies in the University of Edinburgh is endeavouring to collect, by the much more efficient medium of the tape recorder, the last fragments of the rapidly dying tradition. The Gaelic language is seriously threatened by all the forces that are putting at risk minority cultures all over the world; even so, it is astonishing that so much has survived into the twentieth century of a language and its traditions which springs directly from that spoken by an ancient Celtic people whose culture was archaic long before the English ever set foot in Britain and which the Romans must have found so strange on their rare, exploratory trips to Ireland.

In order to understand anything of the formative elements that have gone into making Gaelic Scotland into a distinctive cultural unit, it is necessary to glance briefly at the early history of the country and the nature of the various peoples who inhabited it. The area covered in the book is huge and varied. It includes districts which were at one time Gaelic-speaking and, at an earlier period, were inhabited by Welsh- or Pictish-speaking peoples; regions which were Gaelic-speaking until comparatively recent times, and territory where the Gaelic language is still in everyday use to some extent or another. It includes areas which have had a totally different historical evolution from each other, where external influences of different types and of differing degrees have operated, and in which the religions have been, and still are, very mixed.

In Roman times a people known as the Caledonii occupied land extending from the Valley of the Tay to the Great Glen. Two place-names in Perthshire still bear witness to the presence of these people – the mountain Shiehallion on the Moor of Rannoch, 'the Fairy Mound of the Caledonians', about which has accrued much legend, and another hill, Dunkeld, 'the Fort of the Caledonians'. The original Caledonian confederacy included many other tribes; the Taezali of the far north-east; the Lugi of Sutherland; the Decantae of Easter Ross, the Smertae between the Lugi and the Caereni of north-west Sutherland. These powerful Caledonians constituted a strong threat to the Romans and constantly harassed them and raided into territory which they had occupied further south. Scots from Ireland came in their ships and raided the western coasts; the Picts from northern Scotland also joined in the attacks. The Caledonii spoke a language which was the ancestor of Welsh, that is, British; the Picts used a speech containing an admixture of elements including British. Their language has not, as yet, been satisfactorily deciphered. By the end of the fifth century AD Scotland had become a land, not of seventeen or so tribes, but of four kingdoms. The largest of these was that of the Picts, extending from the Forth to the Pentland Firth; they were divided into the northern and the southern Picts until eventually they became amalgamated into one kingdom.

The second people are the people who most concern us here – the Scots, for they gave the Gaelic language to Scotland, and the name to the country. They came from Ireland to the west coast of the Highlands bringing with them their peculiar form of the Celtic language; Scotland means the lands of the *Scotti* or Scots. They settled in Dalriada (Argyllshire and the adjacent islands), naming it after their own territory in Ireland. It is of some importance to note that the Irish settlers were not pagans, as were the three other peoples who occupied Scotland at that time, but Christian, although many pagan traditions still lurked beneath their Christianity, as they have done down to the present day. And, although Dalriada was the smallest of these kingdoms, it was from this Gaelic settlement that the first king of a united Scotland came. The third people were the Britons of Strathclyde, and the fourth kingdom was that of the Angles, whose territory reached as far as the Firth of Forth.

These four kingdoms were constantly at war with each other, but the conversion of the three pagan factions to Christianity made ultimate union possible. In 843 Kenneth MacAlpin became King of the Picts as well as ruler of the Scots; any threat from Anglian power had been destroyed in 685 at the Battle of Nectan's Mere in Angus. Kenneth MacAlpin extended the boundaries of his territory, but he could never finally conquer the Angles and he remained King of Alba as the united kingdoms were called. It was not until the victory of Malcolm II at the Battle of Carham in 1018 that total victory came to the Scots, and the four peoples became united under Malcolm's grandson, Duncan I and Scotland came into being. This did not include Orkney and Shetland, or parts of Northern Scotland and the Hebrides which were at that time under Norse rule — another important cultural factor influencing the subsequent development of Highland history and its traditions.

It is at the boundaries between Gaelic and non-Gaelic areas that some of the most interesting folk material is to be found, for traditions pay no respect to geography, and there must always be some peripheral region where they mingle and blend into each other. Settlements too, of one people into the territory of another group, can cause the introduction of stories and traditions which rightly belong to a different district or milieu. But, even so, there is a fascinating universality and consistency in the legends and superstitions in the Highland areas of Scotland, in spite of the

Pictish symbols

different influences and ideas that have been introduced at some stage or another down the centuries. The result of all this amalgam of cultural influences and chance contacts down the ages is well-expressed by John Campbell in his introduction to his *Popular Tales of the West Highlands*:

> In the islands where the western wanderers settled down and where they have remained for centuries, old men and women are still found who have hardly stirred from their native islands, who speak only Gaelic, and cannot read or write, and yet their minds are filled with a mass of popular lore, as various as the wreck piled on the shores of Spitzbergen.

Using the quern

Highlander

―――― 2 ――――

Clan Lore

IN ORDER to fully understand the nature of surviving tradition in Gaelic Scotland, social, as well as historical factors must be taken into account. Until the final breakdown of the clan system in the eighteenth century, after the disastrous Battle of Culloden in 1746, Highlanders were organised in tribes or clans (from *clann,* 'children'), as were the Celts from time immemorial. After the defeat of Prince Charles Edward Stuart by the Duke of Cumberland and his troops, this ancient system ceased to function officially, although it has survived vestigially until the present day, having acquired a certain glamour with the establishment of Balmoral as a royal residence and the interest of the Royal family in things Highland.

Nearly all the Highland clans traced their origins back to Ireland; genuine clan names appear in the tenth, eleventh and twelfth centuries. Most of the genealogies are traced back to Loarn, son of Erc, one of the three brothers who established the kingdom of Dalriada in Argyllshire in the late fifth century AD. The Lords of the isles, the MacDonalds, however, trace their ancestry back to

Colla Uais of Ireland. The Campbells seem to have a purely fictitious origin, and the MacLeods and Nicholsons have a strong Norse element in their genealogy. The concept of *clan* differed from that of *tribe* in that the central feature of the clan was consanguinity or kinship; that of the tribe, *tuath*, had a territorial basis. As the word *clann* means 'progeny, children', the members of any clan, from the chief down, were bonded together by blood relationship, the degree of which varied; the chief of the clan and the heads of the various branches or *septs* were closely related, but there were, of course, accretions to the clan who could, strictly speaking, claim no blood relationship. But the clansmen bore a common name, and this name was derived from a common ancestor who may, in certain instances, have been a pagan deity rather than a historical character. In the later Middle Ages, the feudal system was extended in Scotland and the clans were confined to the more inaccessible districts; and, as we have seen, this archaic system lasted until the eighteenth century, when it was ended as a result of Culloden Moor. The chief was believed — like the old pagan kings — to be semi-divine, in that he could do no wrong and loyalty to him was absolute. The clan chief was the real owner of the clan territory; the clansmen got their land from him and in return they gave him goods in kind and military service. Early records make it clear that the clan as a functioning organisation in Scotland existed as early as the sixth century AD. If a clansman had to obey a feudal superior and his orders were at variance with those of his chief, then the feudal lord, or king, would be ignored; when the clans were sufficiently isolated to make punishment for this too difficult to enforce, then they could escape retribution.

For this reason, the Western Highlands and Islands were, for centuries, ruled by petty sovereigns and the king's writ simply did not apply. Inter-clan relations tended to be bad — like inter-tribal strife in ancient Gaul and Ireland — and this had tragic consequences for Highland history. The story is one of petty jealousies, bitter quarrels, constant raiding of land and plundering of goods, cattle and women, and many atrocities were committed by all parties. The clan was by no means a democratic organisation; like all Celtic society, it was highly aristocratic. The various offices were hereditary; the chief was the commander of the clan in war; the oldest member of the cadet branch was lieutenant-colonel; he commanded the right wing. The youngest member of the cadet branch commanded the rear. Every head of a distinct family was captain of his own tribe. Every clan had its standard-bearer, likewise a hereditary post. Every chief had his poet or bard, to praise him in life and to lament him in death. The bag-pipe was the military instrument for war-music and also much favoured in the chieftains' residences. The pipers were instructed in special piping-schools; one of the most famous of these was that of the MacCrimmons, pipers to the MacLeods of Dunvegan, with their school at Borreraig nearby. Each clan had a special place of meeting; people were summoned to it in times of emergency by the Fiery Cross. Two men, each carrying a pole with a cross of fire-blackened wood attached to the end, ran through the clan territory shouting the military slogan of the clan; if they tired, another took their place. Everyone would arm at once and go to the traditional meeting-place to take orders from their chief. Every clan had a special war-cry; for example, the Grants shouted 'Stand fast Creageallachaidh', the Camerons, 'Sons of Dogs come hither and you shall get flesh', and so on. Every clan had a distinguishing badge; the notion that the clans were recognisable to each other by their gaudy individual tartans is a modern one; they were known by their badges, which were plain and worn in their bonnets. The MacDonalds, for example, wore heather, which was also their war-cry (*fraoch*); the Grants fir; the MacIntoshes holly. To a certain extent the choice of badge would be determined by what was available in a given locality, but it is likely that the plant chosen would have a magical and evil-averting significance also.

Omens were very much regarded when the clan was leaving on some foray — another ancient Celtic custom; it was a good omen, for example, to meet an armed man. If a bare-footed woman crossed the path in front of them, she was seized and blood drawn from her forehead to avert evil. If a deer, fox, hare or some other game animal was seen and not killed, it was an ill omen. There was also a clan custom known as *cuid-oidhche*, 'a night's share or portion'. This was provided for the chief, when he was going hunting or on a raid by the tenant who lived near the hill or place he reached by nightfall and consisted in hospitality for the lord and his men and food for his dogs and horses for one night.

Martin Martin, living in the decades before the clan system

became redundant, has some interesting details to add to our knowledge of its operation. He records that every heir or young chieftain was obliged to give a public exhibition of his valour before he was owned and declared leader of his people who, if satisfied, then vowed to follow and obey him. This again is an archaic custom of initiation rite with its origins far back in the Celtic world. Writing in 1703, Martin notes that he had heard no instance of this practice for some 60 years. He says that a heap of stones in the shape of a pyramid was erected. The young chieftain-elect was placed on this and his friends and followers stood in a circle about him; his elevated position signified his authority over them. One of his oldest friends then handed to him the sword worn by his father and a white rod was given to him at the same time; the giving of the white rod as a symbol of authority is also found in the earliest Irish traditions. Then the chief Druid (as Martin calls him) or orator stood beside the cairn and eulogised the ancestry and noble deeds of the family and its magnificent traditional generosity – a virtue always highly prized by the Celts. Martin also notes that when any chieftain went on a military expedition, blood was drawn from the first animal met with on enemy territory and some of this was then sprinkled on the colours; this was considered to be a good omen. There was always a sentry on top of their houses in Barra, even in Martin's time, called Gockmin (Cockman). Before the clan engaged in battle the chief bard addressed the army, exhorting them to courage and praising the prowess of their forebears. In similar fashion, two ancient Celtic warriors about to engage in single combat would revile their enemy and eulogise their own ancestors. When the bard had completed his oration the men would give a great shout and rush into the fray. Martin says that this speech was known as *Brosnichiy Kah* (*Brosnachaidh Catha*), 'Incentive to Battle'. He records that every great family in the isles had a chief Druid who foretold future events and decided all causes. It is against the broken remnants of this once-rigid clan structure that the extant traditions of the Highlands must be viewed, and clan legends form a major tale type. A few stories from this huge repertoire are given as examples, many of which can still be heard today.

One of the most famous clan legends, which is based on a real event, is that of the Eigg massacre. In 1577, 350 MacDonalds – men, women and children – were allegedly suffocated in a cave in the island of Eigg by the MacLeods; the brutality of this murder shocked even the tough Highlanders, accustomed as they were to violence and brutal death, and the story has remained in the oral repertoire of the islanders. Bones were found in the cave as recently as 1800, while contemporary accounts testify to the truth of this incident.

There are many stories extant about the more famous clan battles, some of which have given rise to proverbial sayings. One of these concerns the Battle of the North Inch which took place at the end of the fourteenth century. The MacIntoshes were a powerful clan and were known as the Clan Chattan. In the fourteenth century they owned the greater part of Badenoch; their crest was the cat, their motto 'Touch not the Cat Gloveless'. A feud developed between them and the Clan Kay; the Earls of Crawford and Moray, by commission, attempted to reconcile them, but failed. They then proposed that 30 men from either clan should meet in the North Inch of Perth and decide the quarrel by the sword in the presence of the king, Robert the Third and all the nobles. In 1396, when they met on the appointed day, one of the Clan Chattan was absent; a smith from Perth, known as Henry Gow, or Hal o' the Wynd, offered to take his place for the sum of seven shillings and sixpence. It was a fierce battle. Twenty-nine of the Clan Kay were killed; the thirtieth man escaped by swimming across the Tay. Nineteen of the Clan Chattan perished. Their victory was due to the phenomenal strength and courage of the Perth smith (always a craftsman held in high esteem in the Celtic regions); as a result a local proverb came into being 'He did very well for his own hand, as Henry Gow did'. His descendants became known as *Sliochd a' Ghobhair Chruim*, 'the Progeny of the Stooping Smith' and they were incorporated into Clan Chattan.

Cattle-raiding was one of the favourite pastimes of the Highlanders, and this led to many a clan battle and bitter feud. Certain characters became famed throughout wide areas for their skill in raiding and evading capture. One of these was Auchry Malcolm of Poltalloch. He was known as Big Auchry and was the best swordsman in the entire countryside. The cattle-raiders were all terrified of him. The MacFies of the island of Colonsay habitually came to lift cattle from Argyll, and Big Auchry was their sworn enemy. The hero used to wear a helmet and a coat of mail, according to tradition. He made a little bothy or hut for himself on the hill above his home at Baile-ghuirgean; he taught his dog not to bark, but to warn him of approaching strangers by scratching his ear. One day the MacFies surprised and killed the dog. Before he died he managed to bark a warning to his master, who advanced upon the MacFies and killed many of them. In the end, however, their superior numbers prevailed and Big Auchry was slain.

Another story is told as to how the Camerons got their clan slogan. Lochiel and the Duke of Athol had a dispute about the ownership of Aird-Raineach; they frequently met and argued about the possession of this piece of land and often came to blows, but no decision. They agreed to meet alone, without their followers, at Aird-Raineach and fight it out between themselves. It was also agreed that each of them would take his own piper. Lochiel met the famous witch Gormla as he set out on his journey; she warned him that Athol meant treachery and advised him what to do. He took his men and kept them hidden until he should make a certain sign; the Duke had likewise hidden his men, and when they emerged, so did Lochiel; the Camerons (Lochiel's clan) were victorious. From this encounter the slogan and the Cameron pipe tune are said to have originated:

> Come hither, Come hither,
> You shall get flesh, you shall get flesh.
> Come Sons of hounds, you shall get flesh,
> You shall get flesh.

One tradition pertaining to the clan system concerns the lands of Arrochar which were the property of Lord Lennox, who lived at Dumbarton. He owned the lands of Kilmarnock, and the territory from the River Clyde to the region of Kilpatrick, and the lands between Loch Lomond, the Clyde and Loch Long known locally as the 'Isle' above Leven; his extensive territory came within sight of Loch Fyne and extended as far north as the northern end of Loch Lomond. In the east, they bordered on the lands of the notorious MacGregors, at Inversnaid. The rich lands of Lennox were much plundered by their cattle-raiding neighbours. There were no proper roads, only footpaths, and whenever he could, Lord Lennox travelled by boat. If freebooters passed through the territory with

loot from other clan lands tribute used to be extracted from them
(*staoigcreiche*); the laird of Arrochar had a watchman who used to
keep guard from the top of Stronafian; his house was called *Tigh a'
bheachdachain*, Watchman's House, and can still be seen at the
roadside at the foot of Stronafian. Legends of Norse raids into the
lands of Lennox were current until recent times; one tells of a king
of Norway who once invaded Scotland. He allegedly sailed up
Loch Long with a fleet and landed at a point close to where
Arrochar Castle now stands. He and his followers dragged their
ships from Loch Long to Loch Lomond. A battle ensued and the
men of Arrochar were defeated. The Norwegians then sailed down
Lomond to Luss and many people were slaughtered. The day of the
battle was remembered locally as the Black Monday of Arrochar.

Clan legends are to be found all over the Highlands. One
concerns Cameron free-booters from Sunart who carried off spoil
from Lennox again. MacFarlane, laird of Arrochar, was at that time
the official guardian of the lands of Lennox. He sent his officer,
Calum Garbh MacEwen with a party of men in pursuit of the spoil.
Calum had a clever lad with him – a very popular theme in Gaelic
stories. The boy cut a brier and fashioned it into a walking stick. He
overheard a conversation by the men of Sunart concerning the
stolen beasts. It was decided that the lad should pretend to have the
second sight and should appear to find the stolen cattle by
supernatural means. Calum Garbh quartered his men in Sunart, after
complaining to the laird about the theft and pretended that he could
not trace the cattle. He told his Cameron hosts however that his boy
had magic powers and could find them by means of the rod which
he held in his hand. The boy is of course able to find all the booty
and the laird of Sunart had to pay for the total number of cattle
lifted.

Another legend pertaining to Arrochar tells how MacFarlane of
Arrochar was once grazing a herd of cattle on Ben Voirlich; the
herd was stolen. MacFarlane sent Calum Garbh MacEwen and a
band of men in search of the thief and the cattle. They went north of
Inverness and one night, in a wood, they heard a drunken man
singing:

> I took booty from Ben Voirlich,
> When the people were sleeping;

I gained much wealth for them:
It is a joy to me to mention it.
Some I spent on crowdie
And some on oat-cake;
I would not complain of my foray
Had not my boots become hard.

The Arrochar men seized the thief and recovered their cattle; treachery, if it was clever, was never rejected by the lawless Gaels and the thief was told that if he handed over the beasts, or the money he had got for them, they would not hang him. When he had complied, they did proceed to hang him, not for the crime he had committed, as they had promised, but in order to make sure that he could never repeat it! Under the clan system, life cannot have differed much from life in the Iron Age in Britain, when tribe warred against tribe, the fittest and cleverest members of a community survived, and when cattle-raiding and stories telling of the skill and adventures of the raiders were the normal, everyday pursuits.

One late clan story, also concerning Arrochar and the rich lands of Lennox which were such a temptation to raiders, tells of an episode that is alleged to have taken place a short time after the adventures of Prince Charles Edward Stuart. A farmer called James Turner lived in Arrochar about two miles from the head of Loch Long. He was rich both in cattle and in money. Some of his relations lived in Sunart. One of these planned to go with a group of men and rob him. It was in the spring of the year and they reached Turner's house just before daybreak; the people of the house were already up. Men, known as Sturdy Beggars used, at the time, to go from house to house, begging for alms. One of these had been telling the farmer and his family stories all night long – a common enough phenomenon in the Highlands, and such itinerant men had a great store of tales and traditions. The farmer's wife had a big pot of water boiling over the fire. A fight broke out between the raiders and the farmer's people; the Sturdy Beggar was the best fighter of all, but he fell, and the farmer himself was badly-wounded. The Sunart men made a hole in the door and put their gun-muzzles through, but the farmer's wife poured boiling water on them making them useless. A neighbour ran to the minister. He put on his kilt and armed himself with gun and sword. The fiery cross was sent out through Arrochar and the war-cry 'Loch Sloy' called. The men of the countryside were immediately armed and the raiders fled. The men were caught and sentenced to slavery on a man of war, but they managed to escape and fled back to Sunart.

There is a huge repertoire of legend about individual clans, and a large number of tales about famous or notorious characters belonging to some clan or other. One of the best-known of these is the wild Rob Roy MacGregor round whom a huge body of folklore has developed. Before the Rising of 1745, Highland gentlemen used to run schools in order to instruct the youth of their own district in swordsmanship. The boys were given bannocks and cheese, and they had to run up a hill to eat these. Charles, the son of Stuart of Ardshiel, was educated in Aberdeen. After a long period of education, the boy could still neither read nor write. Ardshiel was going to thrash the boy, but he prevented him because he confessed that he had not been learning education, but the arts of war, which greatly pleased the father. When Ardshiel was dead, Charles went to Lanark to seek the hand of the daughter of the laird there. As he and his men were crossing the moor a vicious bull was let loose on them. Charles killed the bull with his sword, and he and his companions continued on their journey. The laird of Lanark refused to give his daughter to young Ardshiel, and the men set off for home via Balquhidder and they stopped at an inn there. Rob Roy MacGregor heard that they were there. He went to see them and they began to drink whisky together. When they were somewhat drunk they began to talk of the battle of Sheriffmuir; Rob began to criticise the men of Appin for their part in it. A furious argument developed and the two men agreed to meet and fight at sunrise next day. The sun was shining in Charles' eyes; he cut Rob's ear; Rob was then cut in the throat and the fight ended. Rob stated that Charles was the best swordsman he had ever encountered — high praise from the notorious MacGregor. The laird of Lanark was so pleased to hear that Charles had worsted Rob that he gave him the hand of his daughter after all. Rob entertained them. He died shortly after that and he gave orders before his death that the men of Ardshiel were not to be molested.

Another story which took its place in the great body of Gaelic oral lore concerns the Battle of Clachnaharie in 1454. This fight was between the MacIntoshes and the Munroes. John Munro was returning to the Highlands from Edinburgh with his followers. They rested in a meadow in Strathardle and fell asleep. The owner of the land, resenting their intrusion, had the tails of their horses cut off — a bitter insult. He went home, and returned to Strathardle with 350 men and laid waste to it and drove away the cattle. As he was passing Loch Moy in Strathearn he was noticed by MacIntosh of Moy who sent to ask him for the fee that was his due, for it was a custom among the Highlanders that when any spoil of cattle was driven through a gentleman's land, he should be given a proportion of the spoil. Munro offered what he thought was a fair amount, but it was less than that requested. MacIntosh, annoyed by what he took to be an insult to his emissary, gathered a body of men, pursued the Munroes, and at Clachnaharie near Inverness a fierce battle was fought. Men were slain on either side, including Moy himself. John Munro was lamed and was ever after known as *Iain Bacach*, 'Lame John'.

These are but a few examples of one type of tale told widely in the Highlands long after the lawless and wild clan system had disintegrated, stories much relished by the people whose immediate ancestors were concerned in the exploits and battles that formed the everyday life of the Gaels down the centuries.

Trio of gods

⟹ 3 ⟸

Seers and Second Sight

THE HIGHLANDERS have always been famed for their gift, real or alleged, of the 'Sight', and controversy on this subject has been widespread and heated. Martin Martin describes it as a singular faculty of foreseeing events and objects which are invisible to those without this power. The things seen were usually of a doleful or unpleasant nature; the problem was well-known to Charles Churchill, and in his poem, *The Ghost,* he speaks knowledgeably, if astringently, of this acknowledged gift. He says:

> Among the rest, in former years,
> Campbell, illustrious name appears,
> Great Hero of futurity,
> Who *blind* could ev'rything *foresee,*
> Who *dumb* could ev'rything *foretell,*
> Who, Fate with equity to sell,
> Always dealt out the will of Heaven,
> According to what price was given.

Of *Scottish* race, in Highlands born,
Possess'd with native pride and scorn,
Campbell foretold, just what he would,
And left the stars to make it good;
On whom he had impress'd such awe,
His dictates current pass'd for Law;
Submissive all his Empire own'd;
No Star durst smile, when CAMPBELL frown'd.

Seers were no new phenomenon in Celtic society in Churchill's day. They were a flourishing and influential element in society in Caesar's time, as he and other classical writers on the Celts record. They formed a powerful section of the highly-aristocratic population in the early Celtic world, and perhaps, like Churchill's Campbell, charged highly for their services. They were called Vates by the Romans, literally 'seers' or 'prophets'. They had a certain religious power, not as great as that of the Druids, the famous pagan Celtic priests, but ritual certainly formed part of their functions. It took some twenty years to become a Druid, and about twelve years to be a qualified *filed*. Modern seers have an easier time of it; they use their natural gifts without special training. Most people who have 'the Sight' fear it; their neighbours in the townships which stud the Highlands and Islands do not like it either, lest some bad news concerning themselves should be foretold. Some people have the complete gift of Second Sight; others have it in a limited way; for example, they can see things that are to happen to some individual in dreams. When such people say they have been 'dreaming' about someone, the person concerned would usually prefer not to know the nature of the dream, as it frequently forebodes ill. In the Highlands, the person seeing the vision is known as a *taibhsear*, the object seen, *taibhs*, and the act of seeing *taibhsearachd*. Second Sight was, and still tends to be, implicitly believed in the Highlands and Islands of Scotland. Martin Martin wrote a special booklet on the phenomenon, and even the sceptical Dr Johnson had belief in it. Boswell tells us:

He enquired here (Skye) if there were any remains of the second sight. Mr M'Pherson, Minister of Slate, said, he was *resolved* not to believe it, because it was founded on no principle. — Johnson:

'There are many things then, which we are sure are true, that you will not believe. What principle is there, why a loadstone attracts iron? why an egg produces a chicken by heat? why a tree grows upwards, when the natural tendency of all things is downwards? Sir, it depends upon the degree of evidence that you have.' Young Mr. M'Kinnon mentioned one M'Kenzie, who is still alive, who had often fainted in his presence, and when he recovered, mentioned visions which had been presented to him. He told Mr M'Kinnon that at such a place he should meet a funeral, and that such and such people would be the bearers, naming four; and three weeks afterwards he saw what M'Kenzie had predicted. The naming the very spot in a country where a funeral comes a long way, and the very people as bearers, when there are so many out of whom a choice may be made, seems extraordinary. We should have sent for M'Kenzie, had we not been informed that he could speak no English. Besides, the facts were not related with sufficient accuracy. Mrs M'Kinnon, who is a daughter of old Kingsburgh, told us that her father was one day riding in Sky, and some women who were at work in a field on the side of the road, said to him, they had heard two *taiscks* (that is, two voices of persons about to die,) and what was remarkable, one of them was an English *taisck*, which they never heard before. When he returned, he at that very place met two funerals, and one of them was that of a woman who had come from the main land, and could speak only English. This, she remarked, made a great impression upon her father.

The most famous seer in the last few centuries was the so-called Brahan Seer, Coinneach Odhar Fiosaiche, 'Sombre Kenneth of the Prophecies', Kenneth MacKenzie, who lived according to tradition in the seventeenth century. He was born at Uig in the Island of Lewis in the Outer Hebrides. The story of how he got the stone which enabled him to determine the future is as follows. His mother was at the shieling (hill-grazing) and was keeping her eye on the cattle one night, round about midnight, on a hill overlooking an ancient burial-ground. She suddenly saw that all the graves were opening in it and their occupants emerging from them and going off in all directions. After about an hour they returned and re-entered their tombs, and the graves closed over them again. The woman noticed that one grave alone remained open. With great courage she went to the grave and placed her distaff over it, because it was believed that, being of rowan wood, the spirit could not enter the grave while it was there. Soon she saw a beautiful woman who rushed at her and demanded that she should remove her stick from the grave. The mother refused to do this until the occupant of the grave told her why she came back so much later than the others. The spirit told her why she came back so late; she was a daughter of a king of Norway who had been drowned near the island and her body recovered from the nearby beach. While she was released from the grave she had gone back to Norway to look at her old home. As a result of the woman's courage, the spirit gave her instructions on where to find a small, round, blue stone which would empower her son to foresee future events. This she must give to the boy.

As soon as he received the stone, Kenneth began to make prophecies, and he soon became famous in the west. He had been born on Seaforth territory and so was closely connected with the MacKenzies of Seaforth. When the family moved to Loch Ussie on the Brahan estate in Ross-shire he went with them. There are various other traditions as to how Kenneth obtained the magic stone of knowledge. Some versions of the legend maintain that the stone was white, others hold that it was blue; in some traditions, it had a hole in the centre and this is in keeping with the widespread belief that magic stones were holed. Some of the Brahan Seer's prophecies became widely famed in the Highlands and it is maintained that almost every one, except one, has come true to date, and that the last will eventually be fulfilled. It is one of his prophecies, which was made 150 years before the Caledonian Canal was constructed, that ships would sail round the back of Tomnahurich Hill (the Hill of the Yew-trees) at Inverness. This is of course remarkable, and it seemed to be completely impossible at the time. Apparently, when an Inverness man, who was recording Kenneth's prophecies from oral tradition, heard this one, he thought it so ridiculous that he destroyed his manuscript believing the whole thing to be a fraud. The Seer also prophecied the clearance of the Highlands to make way for sheep and deer forests, and he foretold the breakdown of the clan system. He said there would be a white house on every hillock, and this is taken to mean the shooting lodges that came to be scattered all over the Highlands, although there was, of course, no thought of them in Kenneth's day. One of his most remarkable prophecies was, again, about Tomnahurich (also called Tom-na-Sithichean, 'The Fairies Hill'). He said the day would come when the hill would be under lock and key and the fairies which were alleged to inhabit it would be secured within. He could have had no knowledge that a large cemetery would be built there long after his death. The chained fairies would be the spirits of the dead (as they are often alleged to be); there is a strong link between the fairy 'host' and the souls of the departed according to Celtic belief. The hill was not, in fact, turned into a cemetery until after 1859. One prophecy, as yet unfulfilled, was that the Island of Lewis would be destroyed by a violent battle which would continue until the contending parties, after great losses on both sides, reached Tarbert in Harris. After this event, there was to be a great period of peace for Lewis; this kind of prophecy evidently refers to clan warfare, and so seems unlikely to be realised now.

Many of these prophecies can still be heard in the Highlands, where the name of the Brahan Seer is legendary. Kenneth prophesied that a loch above Beauly would burst its banks and the flood would destroy a nearby village, and, although that has not yet come about, people were concerned about it even as recently as the present century. He also made a prophecy about Clach-an-t-Seasaidh (a standing stone), near the Muir of Ord. This stone orginally stood upright to a considerable height, and was pointed at the top. Now it lies broken on the ground. According to one version of the legend about its destruction, the Seer said that the day would come when ravens would gorge themselves on the blood of the Clan MacKenzie from the top of the stone after a violent battle which would be fought on the Muir of Ord. He also said that the MacKenzies would be so decimated after this fight that the remainder of the clan would be taken over to Ireland in an open fishing boat. Ireland was believed to have been their place of origin. In Kintail, this prophecy was applied to the MacRaes, and, up to a point, it has come true in a most unlikely manner. It is thought that Clach-an-t-Seasaidh refers to the remains of a so-called Druidical Circle still visible near Beauly, at a place called Windhill. Another prophecy that has not yet come about concerns a stone pillar again, called Clach an Tiompain, 'The Stone of the Lyre', so-called because of the hollow sound it made in the wind. It is near the famous

Strathpeffer wells, and when it is struck, it makes a great, hollow echoing sound. Kenneth the Seer said that the day would come when ships would ride with their cables attached to Clach an Tiompain; that, of course, has not yet come about. It would require the building of another canal in the vicinity, or the removal of the stone to some nearby harbour, for example, Dingwall.

Another traditional prophecy concerns an Iron Age fort on Knockfarrel, near Loch Ussie where Kenneth lived, in the Strathpeffer Valley. There is a well there called Fingal's Well, inside the fort ruins; Fionn and his men were often associated with hill-forts. Local tradition has it that this well was used by the fort-dwellers until one day Fingal (the famous Irish hero, Fionn mac Cumhaill) drove them away, put a large stone over the well to keep the waters in control and then jumped over the valley; this is one of the numerous tales of Fingal's famous leaps. After heavy rain, if a stick is struck against the stone, a hollow sound is produced, indicating a cavity below, and water can be seen. The Seer prophesied that if ever this stone should be moved, Loch Ussie would force its way up through the well and flood the valley below so that ships could sail up Strathpeffer and be fastened to Clach an Tiompain; this would occur when the stone should be moved after having fallen three times. It has fallen twice, and is propped up a few steps from the roadside as one approaches the Strathpeffer wells. According to one version of the legend, it was the 'Stone of the Lyre' (Clach an Tiompain) which Fionn placed over the well at Knockfarrel fort. Kenneth MacKenzie's magic stone is locally believed to lie at the bottom of Loch Ussie. He is alleged to have thrown it into a pool, which immediately swelled, and became Loch Ussie. This is a typical story of the origins of some loch or river.

No matter how garbled and conflicting many of the traditions of the seventeenth-century Seer are, there is no doubt his prophetic powers made a deep and lasting impact on the folk mind in the Highlands of Scotland. Kenneth obtained his gift from the possession of a magical stone. People possessed of straightforward Second Sight however, do not require any 'aid' for their vision; it comes upon them at random, and, usually, against their will. They dread their mysterious power, which may suddenly manifest itself at any period of their life – in youth, middle years, or age. It is believed that these people have the power of seeing a person's *dopfelganger* or 'other self'. If a person sees his own ghost then his death is believed to be imminent. If a seer meets with it, it does not necessarily mean the person it represents is to die, although this is often the case. It sometimes happens that a person returning to his township from some journey stands aside to let a funeral procession pass by. He recognises the dead from his relations and goes home to say he is sorry to know that such and such a person has died; sometimes he is made to join the procession and act as a bearer and the supernatural weight of the coffin can throw him down on the ground; he then cannot avoid seeing the actual burial.

The writer has met people with this unhappy gift, and witnessed the veracity of what they 'see', and their distress at this faculty they would wish to lose. The person in question is not dead at the time of the experience, but the premonition of his death by a seer usually means that death will follow soon after. Sometimes this gift would seem to run in families and therefore to be inherited; at others, it can begin suddenly, with no family history of such powers. The appearance of the apparition often indicated what was to befall the person in question. If he was actually in a coffin, or wearing grave-clothes, then his death was near at hand; if he wore ordinary clothes then he would not die for some time. The appearance and behaviour of the apparition would be repeated in detail when the real event occurred. The seer could become unhappily haunted by an apparition and be forced to meet it regularly; he never dared to divulge whose spectre it was. These spectres of the living and the ability to see them constitute a totally different group of supernatural phenomena from ghosts proper, and isolated unnatural experiences. Apparitions of this kind could, on occasion, be actually physically dangerous and attack the living seer. Examples of this extraordinary gift of the Second Sight could be given in great quantities; it seems to be very much a feature of Celtic societies and the tradition of the 'Sight' goes back a very long way, as the traditions of Fionn and his magic power of seeing things in the early Irish repertoire of tales indicates.

Some examples of the things witnessed by people with the gift of Second Sight are as follows. Urine was regarded as a powerful element in combating the supernatural. There is a story on record about a man from the island of Tiree who had the Sight. It was a custom in the island that anyone coming upon a drowned body should turn it over. The seer, coming upon such a corpse, was overcome with fear and ran away, without first moving it as tradition demanded. The body was in due course buried, but the dead man began to haunt the seer and caused him great terror. At last things became so bad that one night the apparition dogged his steps home and then stood between him and his own door, barring his entrance. He shouted desperately to his wife to come and sprinkle the doorposts with urine. When she had done this, the ghost leapt above the door and the man entered his house and was no longer disturbed by the menacing vision. It was believed widely in the Highlands that the dead had the power to lay heavy burdens on the living, and to physically punish the living. It was believed by those with faith in the Second Sight that one should never indulge in too strong wishes. Such wishes could affect a person with the Sight. A person could be fatally wounded by means of his 'double', or spiritual body. There are many tales told of people seeing such spirits and throwing dirks, or other missiles at them, and hitting them; some person, whose 'fetch' they in fact were, would, at that moment, be struck blind. People gifted with the Second Sight were often believed to be capable of telling the appearance of someone's future bride or groom. They could see the *taish* ('appearance') of the woman, sitting beside her husband to be. Death was, however, unfortunately the most common event foretold by *taishers*. Seers could also witness events happening at a distance and see if they resulted in evil or good; i.e. someone's son falls overboard and his father is deeply agitated until he is rescued. He 'sees' the whole episode, which is later confirmed. Glasses which were destined to be used at the feast after a funeral were believed to rattle before someone's death. There are a great number of variants of actual experiences people have had, but they all add up to the basic ability to see the person to die before his death, even that of the seer himself, and to see the fetch or spectre of the living long before his actual death.

People were very superstitious about their boats, and if a seer saw anything untoward near, or in the boats, no one would go near that boat. This is an understandable superstition amongst a people who depended so much on sea transport and fishing. Sometimes a boat would be sold because something had been seen in connection with it; this still pertains to a certain extent in some of the more westerly islands, where the only contact with bigger islands or the mainland can be made by boat, and where fish form an important element in the basic diet. Dogs and horses were widely believed to have powers of 'seeing' superior even to those of the most gifted *taisher*. Both could see ghosts and the 'fetches' of people about to die. Horses are believed to have superior powers of 'seeing' even to dogs. They will refuse to pass a haunted spot, or a place where some violent event, such as a murder has, or is about to, take place. The writer has had direct experience of this phenomenon in the islands, where a horse will refuse to go over a particular bridge or pass an area near a burial ground where turves were cut for the graves. It is a widespread belief in the Highlands that dogs in a house will howl if a member of the household is about to die.

Martin Martin was particularly impressed by the tradition of Second Sight in the Gaelic west and recorded many instances of great value and interest. He describes the Sight as the singular faculty of seeing an otherwise invisible object; he too notes that this faculty is not one that was inherited. According to the information he received on his travels in the Western Isles, if a vision is seen early in the morning, the event 'seen' would take place within a few hours. If at noon, it would occur that same day. If observed in the evening, it may come about that night. When a shroud was seen about a person in one of these visions, it was taken to be a sure sign of approaching death. The time of death or its proximity was judged by the height of the shroud about the person in question. If it was not seen above the middle, death was not to be expected for about a year or longer. As it could often be actually witnessed ascending upwards towards the head, so death was believed to be approaching within a few days, or even hours. Martin himself witnessed many examples of this, and, sceptical man though he was, he could not but be convinced of the veracity of this strange power. One, which was told to Martin shortly before he wrote on the subject, concerned the death of a person known personally to him. The vision was recounted to one or two people only, Martin being one of these. It was told in the greatest of confidence. Martin paid no attention to what he had been told until the person in question died when it had been foretold, and this finally convinced him that there was some truth in the belief. This particular person thereafter became a noteable seer, and in Martin's day lived in the parish of St Mary's, the most northerly parish in Skye. Martin records how he had heard that if a woman was seen standing at a man's left hand, it is an omen that she will be his wife, whether they be unmarried or married to others at the time of the vision. If two or three women are seen at once standing close to a man's left hand, the one next to him would be his first wife and the others would follow suit. Martin noted several instances of this actually coming about in his own time. Seers could often see a man who would visit a house in a short time; they could describe the visitor in detail, even if he was a total stranger. If the seer knew the person in question, he could tell his name and describe his character. Martin himself was 'seen' in this way by seers before he even set foot in a place, and where he and his appearance were totally unknown. Seers could also see gardens, houses and trees in places which were empty of all three; this usually came to pass in the course of time. It was believed that to see a spark of fire fall upon one's arm or breast was a sign that a dead child would shortly be seen in the arms of the person concerned. Martin again notes several recent instances of this in his time.

To see a seat empty when someone sitting in it was alive presages that person's death in the near future. When one who has recently been gifted with the 'Sight' (known as a novice) sees a vision in the night-time when out of doors, and enters the house, as he approaches the fire, he then falls in a swoon. Martin tells how some seers find themselves in a cloud of people bearing a corpse along with them. After such a vision, the seer comes home faint and sweating and describes what he has seen. If there are any people among this supernatural host known to the seer he will tell their names, and also name the bearers, but the corpse is unknown to them in these instances. If several people possessed of the Sight were gathered together, they would not all see the vision at the same time. But it was believed that if a person with the Sight should touch, at the time of seeing the vision, another person also having this dread gift, then he too would see it. This preoccupation with death and all its trappings is very typical of the Celts and goes right back to the ancient widespread cult of the dead and the worship of graves and the ancestors. It is also very much a reflection of the Celtic passion for the tabulation of everything, and listing all things in a fit manner; nothing was left to happen as it would; everything must be explicable and predictable. This again is a very archaic trait in the whole Celtic character. One other method of foretelling death was by means of a cry — a *taisg*, according to Martin; in the Lowlands, he says, this is called a 'Wrath' (wraith?). The seer hears a loud cry out of doors resembling the voice of some particular person whose death it foretells. Martin says he heard of this recently in his own time, in the village of Rigg, Skye. Five women were sitting together in one room and they all heard a loud cry passing by the window. They thought it was the voice of a maid who was in fact one of the group. She reddened at the time, but was not herself aware of this. Next day she developed a fever and died the same week.

According to Martin, future events would manifest themselves by smell. Fish or meat cooking over the fire could be smelt at a time when nothing was cooking; this would occur in a house where such an event was unlikely to come about for several months, the house being unoccupied at the time, but the premonition by smell seemingly always came true. Martin says that children, as well as horses and cows, had the power of Second Sight; a child would cry out when it saw a corpse or vision that could be witnessed by an ordinary adult seer. Martin himself had direct experience of this, being present in a house where a child suddenly cried out for no apparent reason. When he was questioned about this he said he had seen a great white thing lying on a board which was in a corner. No one believed him and thought it was pure imagination until a seer who was present told them that the child was correct; he himself had seen a corpse with a shroud about it, and the board in the corner was to be used as part of the coffin. It was in fact incorporated in the making of a coffin for a person who was in perfect health at the time of the vision. Horses were known to Martin, which had panicked and reared up when they saw sights unseen by ordinary men. At Loch Skeriness in Skye, a horse, fastened by rope on the common grazing, broke his tether and ran frantically up and down for no apparent reason. Two people from the neighbourhood happened to be a little distance from the beast and at the same time they saw a largish gathering of men about a corpse, heading towards the church at Snizort. A few days later, a woman who lived some 13 miles from the church, and belonged to another parish, died. Cows were likewise believed to be able to see such doleful visions; if a cow sees something supernatural while it is being milked it will run away in fright and will not be capable of being pacified for some time after.

Seers are said to be — and this is in fact often the case — melancholy people, given to moroseness on account of their undesirable power. Martin records that the people of the isles in general, the seers in particular, are most temperate people, eating the simplest of foods and that in very moderate amounts. He confirms that seers, both male and female, were not epileptics or given to hysterical fits or any psychological disorders. He says that he knew of no mad people with this gift, nor did any of them commit suicide. It was, moreover, held that a drunk person could not see a vision. Martin's insistence on the normality of people with the Sight is interesting testimony to the truth of their gift. Also, seers were not looked upon as visionaries by their friends; they were generally literate, innocent and well-meaning people; they (unlike Churchill's Campbell) made no money on account of their powers. It was a faculty desired by none, and a great burden to those possessed of it. Martin recounts the tale of a boy whom he knew personally, who frequently saw a coffin at his shoulder and was terrified at this vision. He believed it presaged his own death and this was the meaning given to the uncanny sight by the boy's friends. The boy was a servant in the village of Knockow, Skye, where a seer who lived there told the people that they were mistaken in so interpreting the boy's experience. He told the lad to take the first opportunity that occurred for him to act as bearer of a coffin, even for a few moments. A few days later the opportunity presented itself when one of his acquaintances died. After this, the coffin at his shoulder disappeared, but he still continued to see many that concerned the death of others, at a distance from himself. In Martin's day he was regarded as one of the most accurate seers in the Island of Skye. Another Skye seer, a woman this time, often saw a woman with a shroud up to her waist. She always stood with her back to the seer. Her clothing was identical with that worn by the woman. This vision continued to occur for some time until the woman did something to satisfy her family's worry about this vision. She put on clothes different from her usual garments and, moreover, she wore them back to front. Next day the vision appeared facing her and she realised to her horror that it was in fact herself, her own *dopfelganger*. She apparently died shortly after this.

Visions could be seen by several persons, and the foreseen event did not necessarily come about in their lifetime. The Second Sight is not a recent discovery but is seen by many persons of both sexes in several isles; such people had never communicated with each other by letter or by word. Martin says that it was a much more common phenomenon some twenty years before he wrote; even so, it is remarkable that certain people are still believed to have the power in parts of the Highlands even down to the present day, while stories of past occurrences are legionary.

Martin tells a variety of stories on the basic theme of the vision seen by the seers. One concerns four men who were in Flodigarry, in the Island of Skye again. They were sitting at supper; one of them suddenly let his knife fall onto the table and looked extremely angry. The others asked him what was wrong, but he gave them no answer until he had finished his meal. He then told his companions that when he let his knife fall he had seen a corpse with a shroud wrapped round it, laid on that very table. A few days later a member of that family died and was, in fact, laid out on the table where they had dined. This tale came to Martin at first-hand. Another story concerns a man called Daniel Stewart, who lived in the parish of St Mary's in Skye again. One day, at noon, he saw five men on horseback riding northwards. He ran to meet them, and when he reached the road he could not see any of them, which astonished him. He told his neighbours of this strange occurrence. Next day he saw the same number of men and horses coming along the road, but he felt less inclined to speak to them. They then spoke to him and he realised that what he had seen the previous day had, in fact, been a vision. This was the only supernatural experience he ever had. The riders turned out to be Sir Donald MacDonald and his men who at the time of the vision were some 40 miles south of the seer. Martin tells of a woman in Stornoway, capital of the Island of Lewis in the Outer Hebrides, who had a maid who was given to seeing visions. When these occurred she would faint. Her mistress was very concerned about her, but she could not prevent her from seeing things. At last, she determined to pour some baptismal water on the girl's face in the belief that this would stop her from being troubled by these things. She took the maid to church on the Sabbath and sat with her ear to the basin containing the holy water; before the minister had finished the final prayer she put her hand in the basin, and taking as much water as she could she threw it onto the girl's face. The minister and the congregation were shocked at this seemingly unreasonable behaviour. After the prayer was over, the minister asked the woman why she had acted so strangely. She told the minister of the girl's visions and said she believed that this would put an end to them. The result justified the act, and the maid was no longer troubled by these supernatural happenings. The minister of the place himself testified to this, as did several members of the congregation who had been present.

Another instance of the Sight concerns a man called John Morison, also from Lewis, a person of high integrity, who told Martin that about a mile from his own house a girl of twelve lived, who was much troubled by the frequent sight of a girl who resembled herself in height, dress, and general appearance. When the girl moved, so did the vision, and everything the girl did was done by her fetch. She was very distressed by this, and her parents were terrified. John Morison was consulted and he enquired into the religious training of the girl; finding her to be untaught in this field, he told her parents that she must be instructed in the Creed, the Ten Commandments, and the Lord's Prayer and that she should say the Lord's Prayer daily after her prayers. Mr Morison himself, and her family daily joined in prayers on her behalf. After this, the vision disappeared and she never saw it again. John Morison also told of a man living three miles north of himself, who was likewise much haunted by a spirit which he recognised to be identical with himself. The spirit spoke to him when he was working in the fields, but it never spoke to him in the house, where no one but the haunted man could see it. He was much distressed by this, and confided in one of his neighbours; the neighbour advised him to cast a live coal at the face of the spirit next time it appeared. The man did this on the following day in the presence of his family. However, on the next day, the ghost or fetch appeared to him in the fields again and beat him so severely that he was bed-ridden for fourteen days afterwards (beating by a supernatural being is an ancient Celtic belief). Mr Morison, who was minister of the parish, and several friends came to see the man who was by now very distressed, and they joined in prayer that he should be freed from this terrible affliction. But Martin records that he was still being haunted at the time Martin had to leave the island.

Again, he tells of a man at Knockow in the parish of St Mary's in Skye who was in good health and was quietly sitting in company with his fellow-servants one night, when he was suddenly taken ill, and fell backwards from his seat and began to vomit. Such a thing had never happened to him before and his family were very alarmed. When he recovered from his fit he felt all right. One member of the family had the Sight and told the others that the cause of the man's sudden and severe attack was a very remarkable one. He named an evil woman who lived in the adjacent village of Bornaskittag, whom he had seen approaching the afflicted person in a violent rage; she threatened him with her hands and her head until she caused him to fall over backwards, unconscious. The reason was, the woman in question was in love with her victim and felt she had been slighted in her affections. Once again Martin states he had this information from first-hand sources. Another person living at St Mary's told the minister, a Mr MacPherson, and others that he had seen a vision of a corpse coming towards the church, not by the common road but by a rough way which seemed so unlikely that his neighbours thought he was mad. He told them to wait and see; one of his neighbours eventually died and his body was carried over the ground as the man had witnessed because the road was completely blocked by snow. The minister himself told this to Martin. Another Skye man, Daniel Dow (*Dubh* 'black') from Bornaskittag was frequently bothered by the appearance of a man who threatened to strike him. He did not recognise the man, but he could describe him in detail. About a year after this he had to go to Kyle-Rae some thirty miles south-east of his home. As soon as he got there he saw the man who had threatened to strike him. Within a few hours a quarrel developed, blows commenced, and one of the men was wounded in the head. The seer's master recounted this to Martin on his painstaking efforts to find out the truth about the Second Sight in the West.

Another story tells how some people from the Island of Harris were sailing round the Island of Skye, with the intention of reaching the mainland, when they were astonished to see the apparition of two men hanging down by the ropes that secured the mast. They could not understand what this portended. They continued on their journey, but the wind turned against them and they were forced into Broadford, in the south of Skye. There they found Sir Donald

MacDonald holding court, and the death sentence being pronounced on two men. The ropes and the mast of that same vessel were then used to hang the criminals. Once again, this remarkable story was given to Martin at first-hand. Several people belonging to a certain family told Martin that they had frequently seen two men standing at a young gentlewoman's left hand – the girl was in fact the daughter of their master. They could name the men. Sometime later, they could see a third man standing by her, and this one from then on always stood closest to the girl. The seers did not know the man but they could describe him in detail. Some months later, this man did come to the house and his appearance exactly fitted the description of him given by the servants. And shortly afterwards, he married the young woman.

One strange tale was told to Martin by Sir Norman MacLeod himself, concerning an experience he had had personally. His servant, as Sir Norman related, had an unusual experience in his absence. He went to the Island of Skye on business and did not tell his household on Bernera (which lies between North Uist and Harris) when he would return. His servants, in his absence, were together in the hall one evening and were told by one of their number, who was gifted with the Sight, that they must be off because there would be a large gathering in the hall that night. The others argued with the seer; but within an hour one of Sir Norman's men came to the house and requested lights etc. for the master who had just landed; Sir Norman, hearing of the vision, called for the seer and questioned him about it. The man said he had seen the spirit *Brownie* (see p. 159) in human shape, come several times pretending to carry off an old woman who was sitting by the door. Finally, he appeared to carry her out by the neck and the heels; this had made him laugh. The other servants thought he was mad to burst out laughing without any obvious reason, for they could not see the creature. Sir Norman apparently told Martin this story himself.

Martin also records another story of how the arrival of a stranger was 'seen' in advance of his coming. It concerns the island of Rona which lies some 20 leagues from the north-east point of Ness in Lewis and is about a mile in length and about half a mile in breadth. There is a hill at the western part, and the island can only be seen from Lewis on a clear summer day. Several of the natives of Lewis described the island and its customs to Martin. The minister of Barvas, Mr Daniel Morison, had Rona as part of his glebe and he used to visit it from time to time. The natives had a great affection for him. When he first arrived they greeted him as follows, indicating that his arrival had been foretold by them by means of the Sight. 'God save you, Pilgrim, you are heartily welcome here; for we have had repeated apparitions of your person among us and we heartily congratulate your arrival in this remote country.'

Seers and augurers were then widely believed in in the Highlands, and even today in the Western Isles one can hear tales of people with the Sight, foretelling future events, not always of a gloomy nature, and collect stories of fated boats and doomed fishermen and sailors. Alexander Carmichael, the assiduous collector of such traditions in the last century, recorded a very fine divination. An augurer was known as *frithir,* and the means of divination was called in Gaelic *frith* 'augury'. This enabled the augurer to look into the unseen. The divination was made in order to know where an absent person or lost beast was at any given time, and in what condition. The divination could not be made at any time; it must be performed on the first Monday of the quarter, just before sunrise. The augurer had to fast, and the augury was carried out in the following manner. The seer must go, bare-footed, bare-headed, and with closed eyes, to the doorstep and place a hand on each jamb. He invoked God to show him the unknown. He then opened his eyes and gazed in front of him; he made his divination from the nature and the position of the objects that he then saw. Apart from the Brahan Seer, there were many famous augurers or seers in the Highlands and Islands. One Gaelic legend has it that when Christ was missing, Mary found out that he was in the temple by means of augury. For this reason the following augury was associated with the Virgin and known as *Frith Mhoire,* 'Mary's Augury':

> God over me,
> God before me, God behind me,
> I on thy path, O God,
> Thou, O God, in my steps.
>
> The augury made of Mary to her Son,
> The offering made of Bride through her palm,

Sawest Thou it, King of life?
Said the King of life that He saw.

The augury made by Mary for her own offspring,
When he was for a space amissing,
Knowledge of truth, not knowledge of falsehood,
That I shall truly see all my quest.

Son of beauteous Mary, King of life,
Give Thou me eyes to see all my quest,
With grace that shall never fail, before me,
That shall never quench nor dim.

One of the most beautiful of the old invocations recorded by
Carmichael, in which paganism and Christianity walk amicably
hand in hand, is the *Ora nam Buadh,* The Invocation of the Graces,
It is too long to give in its entirety here, but the more archaic and
beautiful verses are given, in translation from the Gaelic. Carmichael
heard versions of the invocation over a wide area of the islands and
the mainland; the following verses are from a version heard in South
Uist:

I bathe thy palms
In showers of wine,
In the lustral fire,
In the seven elements,
In the juice of the rasps,
In the milk of honey,
And I place the nine pure choice graces
In thy fair fond face,
The grace of form,
The grace of voice,
The grace of fortune,
The grace of goodness,
The grace of wisdom,
The grace of charity,
The grace of choice maidenliness,
The grace of whole-souled loveliness,
The grace of goodly speech.

Dark is yonder town,
Dark are those therein,
Thou art the brown swan,
Going in among them.
Their hearts are under thy control,
Their tongues are beneath thy sole,
Nor will they ever utter a word
To give thee offence.

Thine is the skill of the Fairy Woman,
Thine is the virtue of Bride the calm,
Thine is the grace of Mary the mild,
Thine is the tact of the woman of Greece,
Thine is the beauty of Emir the lovely,
Thine is the tenderness of Darthula delightful,
Thine is the courage of Maebh the strong,
Thine is the charm of Binne-bheul.

Thou art the door of the chief of hospitality
Thou art the surpassing star of guidance,
Thou art the step of the deer of the hill,
Thou art the step of the steed of the plain,
Thou art the grace of the swan swimming,
Thou art the loveliness of all lovely desires.

Peter has come and Paul has come,
James has come and John has come,
Muriel and Mary Virgin have come,
Uriel the all-beneficent has come,
Ariel the beauteousness of the young has come,
Gabriel the seer of the Virgin has come,
Raphael the prince of the valient has come,
And Michael the chief of the hosts has come,
And the spirit of true guidance has come,
And the king of kings has come on the helm,
To bestow on thee their affection and their love.

These gracious, moving lines, recorded in the homes of crofters in the ancient Gaelic language in the remote west of our country, bear striking testimony to the passion of the Celts for learning and beauty, which has always far outstripped their desire for worldly gain and things material. It is an interesting blend of latent pagan concepts, for the love of the old religion has never completely died, with a deep feeling for Christianity; the angel Gabriel is made into a *fàidh*, 'prophet', 'seer'; the Irish divine queen, Maebh (Old Irish Medb) takes her place with dignity beside the Virgin Mary, the Fairy Woman is as deeply respected as the goddess-saint Bride, midwife of the Virgin, according to Catholic tradition in the Hebrides; all the virtues admired by the Celts, and all the animals and birds, sacred down the long ages, are brought into this beautiful incantation.

Invocations played a large part in the folk repertoire of the Scottish Highlands. Sometimes these are of doubtful character, being more obviously pagan than Christian. Others are quite orthodox in their devout Christian feeling. One, invoking God, by its very listing of terrors shows very clearly the superstitious beliefs prevalent at the time. Recorded by Carmichael again, it is called *Beannaich, a Thriath nam Flath Fial*, 'Bless O Chief of Generous Chiefs', where God is likened to the generous chief of the clan, a most important concept for the Highlanders:

> Bless, O Chief of generous chiefs,
> Myself and everything near me,
> Bless me in all my actions,
> Make Thou me safe for ever,
> Make Thou me safe for ever.

Then the dangers are enumerated:

> From every gruagach and ban-shee,
> From every evil wish and sorrow,
> From every glaistig and ban-nigh,
> From every fairy-mouse and grass-mouse.
> From every fairy-mouse and grass-mouse
>
> From every fuath among the hills,
> From every siren hard pressing me,
> From every uruisg within the glens,
> Oh! save me till the end of my day,
> Oh! save me till the end of my day.

Direach of Gleann Eite

These creatures which haunt moor and loch, stream and hill, constitute some of the innumerable supernatural beings which the Gael believed to populate the wild, dangerous country which they inhabited, as closely linked with the otherworld as the world inhabited by their pagan ancestors, who called upon and made sacrifices to the tribal gods by means of similar incantations. Thus much folk belief is inadvertently recorded for posterity in this rich body of material concerning divination and invocation, which was once so prolific in the Gaelic-speaking areas.

Another invocation, where the desired result is believed to be brought about by chanting the correct lines, and having highly-pagan sentiments, occurs in the beautiful *Ora Ceartais*, 'Invocation for Justice'. According to Carmichael, a person seeking justice used to go at dawn to a point where three streams met — always a magic place according to Celtic belief. When the sun shone on the very tops of the hills the man must cup his hands and fill them with water from the point where the streams met. He then dipped his face into his hands, and repeated the Invocation. The more arresting lines are as follows:

> I will wash my face
> In the nine rays of the sun,
> As Mary washed her Son
> In the rich fermented milk.
>
> Black is yonder town,
> Black are those within,
> I am the white swan,
> Queen above them.

> I will travel in the name of God,
> In likeness of deer, in likeness of horse,
> In likeness of serpent, in likeness of king:
> Stronger will it be with me than with all persons.

The swan, and the animals enumerated in these lines are all important in pagan Celtic religious belief; there would seem to be some deep, half-forgotten belief in the metamorphosis and shape-shifting abilities that characterised pagan belief, all being brought under the impeccable aegis of God.

Seers, as well as those not gifted with this peculiar power, had a strong belief in auspicious and inauspicious days, just as did their forebears in the old Celtic world. Carmichael collected many examples of these, one from Christine Gillies of the island of Benbecula, also from Mary MacDonald, Barra, both in the Outer Catholic Isles. A mother had *taibhse*, 'Second Sight'. Her only son grew up and wished to leave the country. His mother was heart-broken at the prospect of his going and thought of every means by which she could prevent it. Knowing her powers of 'seeing', the boy asked his mother what was an auspicious day for his departure. She has 'seen' his death if he carries out his plans, and she answers him in a song which makes this clear:

> You shall not go on Monday nor shall you go on Tuesday,
> Wednesday is tormenting, hurtful,
> On Thursday are temptation, turbulence,
> Friday is a day of rest,
> Saturday is to the Mary Mother,
> Let the Lord's Day praise the High King.
> Thou man who would travel strongly,
> Thou shall not go on Monday, the end of the quarter.
>
> Thou man who would travel lightly,
> There is red blood upon thy shirt;
> Not the blood of roe nor blood of deer,
> But blood of thy body, and thou full of wounds.

So the son stayed with his mother and he was there to close her eyes when her day of death came.

J. G. Campbell, in his *Witchcraft and Second Sight in the Highlands,* says that belief in the Second Sight is specifically Celtic, and in it he would see a remnant of ancient Druidic practice, for the powerful Celtic priesthood were able to foretell events by various signs and omens. He himself does not doubt the veracity of the phenomenon, and makes the point that *Dà-Shealladh* does not really mean 'Second Sight', but 'The Two Sights'. The capacity to see into the world of spirits is reserved specifically for those having this gift. Ghosts of the dead as well as fetches of the living are seen by such people. Most of the events seen refer to the future, even the distant future. The spectres are seen with as much clarity as living beings. He confirms that no one who had this power was envied and that those possessing it regarded it as a heavy burden. He records that it was believed possible to get rid of this dread power. In the island of Coll the people believed that a person afflicted with the Sight could destroy his gift and bind it away from himself (*nasg*) by giving alms (*deirc*) and then praying that it would depart. A seer in Arinagour, Coll, had two sons in the army. They were away on foreign service and he could see by means of his visions how they were faring. What was revealed to him caused him so much distress that he gave money to an old woman and prayed that his Second Sight may be taken away from him. Thereafter, he saw nothing more of his sons. He was very worried about them and so, having lost the gift himself, he went to Tiree to consult a celebrated *taisher* and took the man back to Coll with him. He stood him beside the fire, which at that time was in the middle of the floor of many Highland houses. The best seers always held that visions could be seen most clearly through fire. After a short time, the Tiree seer began to sweat, and the other man knew that this only occurred when the vision was a painful one; he begged the seer to tell him the truth about what he had 'seen' and to keep nothing back from him. The *taisher* said that both the boys had been killed — one by a bullet wound in the head, and the other by a bullet through the heart and neck. Only too soon afterwards the veracity of the seer's vision was confirmed and the two boys were indeed reported as having been shot dead.

The fate of Mary, Queen of Scots had been 'seen' by many Highland seers, as King James notes in his *Demonology.* MacKenzie of Tarbat, later Earl of Cromartie, who was a renowned statesman in the reign of King Charles II, wrote an account of the faculty of Second Sight, and gave the following example of it. He was riding one day in a field where his tenants were manuring barley and a stranger approached the group and said there was no point in their being so busy about their crop, as he saw English soldiers' horses tethered there already. This came true because the horses of Cromwell's army in 1650 ate up that entire field of grain. Another early example of the Sight happened a few years after this, when the Duke of Argyll was playing at bowls with some fellow gentlemen at his castle at Inverary. One of them suddenly turned white and fainted when the Marquis bent down to pick up his bowl. When he came to he cried, 'Bless me, what do I see? My lord with his head off and his shoulders all bloody'. And this, of course, likewise came about.

Pennant, in his journey through Scotland in 1769, records much of interest concerning surviving customs and beliefs. He makes the following statement in explanation of this:

> The country is perfectly Highland (this when he had reached Struan in Perthshire) ... it still retains some of its ancient customs and superstitions; they decline daily, but lest their memory should be lost, I shall mention several that are still practised, or but very lately disused in the tract I had passed over. Such a record will have this advantage when the follies are quite extinct, in teaching the unshackled and enlightened mind the difference between the pure ceremonies of religion and the wild and agile flights of superstition.

He comments that the notion of the Second Sight still prevails in a few places. He also mentions divination by means of an object, in this instance the speal or blade-bone of a shoulder of mutton, well scraped. He records that when Lord Loudon was obliged to retreat before the Rebels to the Isle of Skye, a common soldier, on the very moment that the Battle of Culloden was decided, proclaimed the victory at that distance, pretending to have discovered the event by looking through such a bone. He also records, of the Sight:

> I heard of one instance of Second Sight, or rather of foresight, which was well attested, and made much noise about the time the

prediction was fulfilled. A little after the Battle of Preston Pans, the president, Duncan Forbes, being at his house of Culloden with a nobleman, from whom I had the relation, fell into discourse on the probable consequences of the action: after a long conversation, and after revolving all that might happen, Mr Forbes suddenly turned to a window said 'All these things may fall out; but depend on it, all these disturbances will be terminated on this spot'.

Which of course, came about when the final battle of the 1745 Rising was fought on Culloden Moor in 1746. Pennant records an interesting belief current in his time that the first person, to have the 'sight' according to tradition, was the much-loved Saint Columba, for he foretold the victory of Aidan, King of the Scots, over the Picts and Saxons on the very instant that it came about. He also notes an interesting example of Second Sight told to him when he visited the island of Rum:

> It is not wonderful that some superstitions should reign in these sequestered parts. Second Sight is firmly believed at this time. My informant said that Lauchlan Mac-Kerran of Cannay had told a gentleman that he could not rest for the noise he heard of the hammering of nails into his coffin: accordingly the gentleman died within fifteen days.

Of the same island he says:

> Molly Mac-Leane (aged forty) has the power of foreseeing events through a well-scraped bone of mutton: some time ago she took up one and pronounced that five graves were soon to be opened, one for a grown person; the other four for children; one of which was to be for her own kin, and so it fell out. These pretenders to Second Sight, like the Pythian priestess, during their inspiration fall into trances, foam at the mouth, grow pale and feign to abstain from food for a month, so over-powered are they by the visions imparted to them during their paroxysms. I must not omit a most convenient species of Second Sight, possessed by a gentleman of a neighbouring isle, who foresees all visitors, so has time to prepare accordingly: but enough of these tales, founded on impudence and nurtured by folly.

Collecting examples of custom and belief is one of the most delicate and difficult aspects of fieldwork possible. Highlanders are willing to sing the old songs, recount the ancient proverbs, chant archaic ballads and tell long hero tales. But the question of actual belief is a very personal one, and although an informant may be prepared to say what happened in the Godless past, he will often be unwilling, either for reasons of religion, or for fear of ridicule, or fear that to speak of a thing may bring it about, to admit that the old and powerful superstitions have any remaining meaning for him or his neighbours. Such things tend not to be talked about when strangers are present, and it is remarkable that travellers through the Highlands were able to record deep-rooted beliefs such as the Sight, the Evil Eye, witchcraft and fairy lore at all. Often, of course, their informants were members of the Protestant clergy who frowned on such practices with their deeply pagan undertones, and spoke of them to strangers with scepticism and disapproval.

In Martin Martin's day Skye was much famed for its seers; yet later in the same century Pennant was able to write: 'Very few superstitions exist here at present: pretenders to second-sight are quite out of repute except among the most ignorant and at present are very shy of making boast of their faculties.' And yet the present writer found the island to be full of first-rate examples of custom and belief of every kind, and had direct experience there of people gifted with the unhappy faculty of 'seeing'. Pennant does, however, record a fascinating instance of divination which clearly caused him much amazement. He states:

A wild species of magic was practised in the district of Trotternish, that was attended with a horrible solemnity: a family who pretended to oracular knowledge practised these ceremonies. In this country is a vast cateract whose waters falling from a high rock, jet so far as to form a dry hollow beneath, between them and the precipice. One of these imposters was sewed up in the hide of an ox, and, to add terror to the ceremony, was placed in this concavity; the trembling enquirer was brought to the place, where the shade, and the roaring of the waters, increased the dread of the occasion. The question is put, and the person in the hide delivers his answer. And so ends this species of divination styled *Taghairm*.

This is a method of divination which goes right back to Old Irish tradition, where the priest or seer wrapped himself in a bull-hide, and, upon going into a trance, saw in a vision the answer to whatever question he was asked. Pennant makes mention of the Brahan Seer, and testifies to his fame. Writing of Sutherland, he says:

Every country has had its prophets: . . . Wales its Robin Ddu and the Highlands their Kenneth Oaur. Kenneth long since predicted these migrations in these terms: 'Whenever a Mac-cleane with long hands, a Frazier with a black spot on his face, a Mac-gregor with the same on his knee, and a club-footed Mac-cleod of Rasa, should have existed; whenever there should have been successively three Macdonalds of the name of John, and three Mac-innons of the same Christian name; oppressors would appear in the country, and the people change their own land for a strange one.' The predictions, say the good wives, have been fulfilled, and not a single breach in the oracular effusions of Kenneth Oaur.

and, as another instance of Second Sight observed by Pennant, again writing of Sutherland:

In a country where ignorance and poverty prevale it is less wonderful that a tragical affair should happen . . . about three years ago lived in this neighbourhood, a woman of more than common strength of understanding. She was often consulted on the ordinary occurences of life, and obtained a sort of respect which excited the envy of another female in the same district. The last gave out that her neighbour was a witch; that she herself had a good Genius, and could counteract the evils dreaded from the other; at length she so worked on the weak minds of the simple vulgar, that they determined on destroying her rival, and effected their purpose by instigating a parcel of children to strangle her. The murder was enquired into but the inciters so artfully concealed themselves, that they escaped their reward, and no punishment was inflicted, except what was suited to the tender years of the deluded children.

Fortunately, not many seers and people of exceptional powers received such brutal treatment. In much more recent times, at the end of the last century, long after Pennant recorded that belief in the Second Sight was almost dead in Skye, a strange episode took place, in the house of a gentleman. One evening, round about New Year (a popular season for divination in general), a large number of neighbouring gentry and their families had been invited to a *céilidh* (convivial gathering) at this house; the mistress was away at the time, in the south, and her sons and daughters acted in the role of their mother. After dinner, the young people went to the drawing-room; a quadrille was arranged but before it began the figure of a lady glided along the side wall of the room and was seen by several. One of the girls recognised it to be the form of her mother, and fainted. The vision put an end to the party, and it was later discovered that at the very time the vision had manifested itself, the lady had died in a southern city.

Another strange instance of foresight is recorded from Skye and allegedly happened towards the middle of the last century. The tragic event occurred in the parish of Snizort, where a cottar's wife was delivered of a fine baby. Soon after her birth the mother was visited by the female neighbours, each bringing a gift of fowls, eggs and so on, according to custom. The child was greatly admired, and every good was wished on it. One woman, however, whispered to her neighbour that she was afraid the fine child's life would be short and it would be the cause of terrible grief to its mother. This gloomy utterance made the neighbour very angry. The woman, however, said that she had had a dreadful vision of the little child mangled and bleeding. In a few months time when the child was sleeping in his cradle, the mother left him alone while she went to the well to fetch water. She met a neighbour and they talked for a while; when she reached the house the baby was lying on the floor, torn to pieces. During her absence a fierce pig had wandered into the house and devoured the sleeping infant.

In spite of Pennant's comment, there are many other, comparatively recent examples of the Sight in Skye. One, which happened in the last century again, concerns a parish minister. He went to visit a sick brother of his, a Captain MacLeod, who lived near Portree and had been poorly. This man had a large family. When evening came, the minister mounted his horse and set off for home. This was nine miles away, and before he had been very far a severe storm arose. The minister was an elderly man, and he thought he would be wise to spend the night at Scorribreck rather than attempt to continue with his journey. Mrs Nicolson, mistress of the house, welcomed her guest. She was the person who kept the parish mortuary cloth, as her house was close to the burial-ground. She went to the loft to fetch something and those below heard a scream and the noise of something falling on the upper floor. They rushed up the stairs and found Mrs Nicolson in a fainting fit. When she recovered, she told the minister that she had seen a bright light on the mortuary cloth which was spread out on the table, and in the middle of the light she saw the image of his niece's face, Captain MacLeod's daughter. Shortly afterwards, the girl took ill and died, and that same cloth was used on her bier.

One final example of this strange Highland power of 'seeing' the unseen, again from Skye. Once more a minister is involved, an interesting fact, as the church did not approve of such alleged supernatural powers. Late in the nineteenth century the parish minister visited the miller's house and found the miller's wife in the kitchen, in a very distressed state. Quantities of wood were frequently found on the shore on that area of the island which had drifted in from wrecked vessels. On the day of the minister's visit, the kitchen was full of drift-wood planks, which were drying off there. The woman was extremely glad to see the minister; she said that a well-known seer, Christy MacLeod, had been sitting on one of the planks, by the fire, when she suddenly fainted. She carried her to a bed and laid her on it. The woman begged the minister to go to the seer and ask her about her vision; this he did reluctantly, and without success. However, he persisted and finally she confided in him. She said she had seen a vision while sitting on the plank of wood. She had glanced across at the plank opposite to her and had seen the mangled, bleeding body of a boy, a MacDonald, who, at that time, was in extremely good health. When the minister returned to the miller's house, the woman demanded to know what Christy had seen and he told her. Some six weeks later there was a wedding in the parish to which the boy in question was invited. On his way home alone late at night, he lost his way and fell over a cliff some 1,000 feet high and was dashed to pieces. The body was not found until some days had passed. Men came to the miller's house for a plank on which to place the remains, and the one chosen was in fact the very one on which the seer had seen the vision.

Related to the gift of Second Sight, but somewhat different from it, are certain death-omens which appear in the form of blue, quivering lights. They are seen moving along the course which the funeral procession would take; they could also be seen near the bed of one about to die.

Finally, we shall end this almost inexhaustible aspect of Celtic superstitious belief with the story of a vision seen by several people together, some time after the Battle of Culloden had been fought between Prince Charles Edward Stuart, Pretender to the Scottish throne, and the Duke of Cumberland.

In August 1748, before the Town Council of Aberdeen, eleven men and women swore to the truth of a vision which they said they had seen in a valley five miles to the west of the city. On the fifth of that month, at two o'clock in the afternoon, they saw three globes of light in the sky above, which they first took to be weather-galls but which increased in brilliance until twelve tall men in clean and bright attire crossed the valley. Then were seen two armies. The first wore clothing of dark blue and displayed Saint Andrew's Cross on its ensigns. The other was uniformed in scarlet and was assembled beneath the Union Flag. Twice the red army attacked the blue, and twice it was beaten back. When it rallied and attacked for a third time it was routed and scattered by the Scots army. Those who watched saw the smoke of the cannon, the glitter of steel, and the colours waving, but they heard no sound. When the blue army was triumphant the vision passed.

Antlered god/devil

—◦4◦—

Witchcraft, Black and White

WITCHCRAFT, together with the belief in the power of certain people to bring about a desired situation by magic, is not, of course, confined to the Highlands. But it was, at one time, very prevalent there, and numerous examples of such beliefs are still to be collected from people who claim that they have had direct experience of such things, or who actually know someone with such alleged powers. A distinction is made between black and white witchcraft, and many people embued with powers have, and do, use them for good rather than evil purposes. Amongst these are the 'charmers' or 'healers', men and women who are able either to cure specific ills, or to perform cures in general. The writer has had direct experience of both forms of this power, and the following examples have either been collected personally in the field, or, when taken from written sources, can be paralleled from actual fieldwork material. It is a subject that people are often unwilling to speak about, but there is no doubt that belief in powers to work good and evil is still fairly widespread. Pennant, writing in the eighteenth century, says (of

Breadalbane): 'In this part of the country the notion of witchcraft is quite lost; it was observed to cease almost immediately on the repeal of the witch act.'

But the ancient belief in the malevolent powers of witches was widespread and deep-rooted in the Gaelic-speaking Highlands; and, as we have noted, equal credit was given to the so-called white witches, or 'charmers', people whose alleged supernatural powers were used solely for the good of man and beast. How far these beliefs continue actively into the present day is a matter for speculation; they are subjects which are not readily discussed if any true belief-element is present, but the presence of branches of rowan and horse-shoes nailed above house doors, outside or inside the dwelling, suggest that a certain uneasy credulity lingers on in parts of the Highland area at least. One of the great powers with which witches were accredited was that of the Evil Eye; by merely looking at something they could destroy, corrupt or acquire it. Rowan was held to be a potent talisman against the Evil Eye; and there are extant, even today, charms and incantations to counter the effects of the 'eye'. One, from the Outer Hebrides states:

> I make to thee the charm of Mary,
> The most perfect charm that is in the world,
> Against small eye, against large eye,
> Against the eye of swift voracious women,
> Against the eye of swift rapacious women,
> Against the eye of swift sluttish women.

The witches of Highland tradition are quite distinct from the fairies. Their association with the Devil and the forces of evil was never in doubt; their dark powers could be tapped by those who knew the correct ritual and formulae. Some witches achieved a wide area of fame; others had an essentially local notoriety. Their existence was, however, universally accepted and feared. There are numerous stories of witches and their activities. One of the most typical and famous of these concerns the ruthless Witch of Laggan, in Badenoch. Laggan was one of the three parishes of Badenoch, the other two being Kingussie and Alvie; the district extended from Corryarrick on the west to Craigellachie near Aviemore on the east – some 45 miles of singularly remote and high country. The Witch of Laggan is alleged to have lived two miles from Kingussie, in the seventeenth century. Tales about her can still be heard in the locality. She was famed for her evil deeds and she and her companion witches were both feared and hated. The weird, inhospitable forest of Gaick lies in Badenoch, inhabited only by deer and other wild beasts and birds of prey, and frequented by hunters. Many stories were told of the strange things that happened in this wild tract of country. According to one version of the story of the Witch of Laggan, a local hunter went there one stormy day in search of deer; he was a man of great reputation in the countryside for his hatred of witches and his ruthless persecution of those who practised the Black Art.

On this particular occasion, the storm became extremely violent and he had to make for shelter in his little hut or bothy. He kindled a fire and sat down beside it with his two dogs to wait for the wind to abate. As he sat there, a miserable-looking cat entered the hut — another version has it that it was a hen rather than a cat that came in. The two dogs bristled with terror, their hair stood on end, and then they leapt savagely on the cat. It cried out for mercy, in Gaelic, begging the hunter to call off his dogs and saying that it had need of his protection because it was a poor, wretched witch who had renounced her ungodly habits and, as a result, had been viciously attacked by her companion witches. She had fled to the renowned hunter for protection, knowing his hatred of witchcraft. The man believed her. He called off his frenzied dogs and told the cat to come near the fire and warm itself. Before she would do so, however, she took a long hair and told him to tie the dogs to the beam of the little house with it, or else they would molest her. The hunter pretended to do as she asked, but he only tied the hair round the beam, leaving the dogs free. The cat then approached the fire, sat down, and began to swell. The hunter remarked to it, 'You are getting very large'. 'Oh, yes,' said the cat, 'my fur gets fluffy as it dries in the heat.' But the cat went on steadily increasing in size until it was as big as a big dog and then, in the blink of an eye, there stood a woman. And to the amazed hunter's utter horror he recognised her as a close neighbour of his, a woman of excellent reputation, known locally as the 'Good Wife of Laggan'. 'Hunter of the Hills', said she, 'Your hour has come; you have been the devoted enemy of my persecuted sisterhood for too long. The chief opponent of our order is now dead – this morning I saw him drowned. And now, Hunter of the Hills, it is your turn.'

She then flew at his throat in a fury of hatred; but the dogs, which she supposed to be tied by the magical hair, leapt on her breast and throat. She screamed out to the hair, 'Fasten, fasten', and it tightened its hold on the beam so violently that it snapped the wood into two pieces; but the two dogs remained free. She then tried to escape, but the dogs fastened onto her and tore off one of her breasts and badly-mutilated her. At last, with terrible shrieks the witch took on the form of a raven and flew in the direction of her home. The poor dogs were mortally wounded and died at their heart-broken master's feet; he buried them with as much grief as he would his children and then made his way back home. His wife was out, but soon after his return she came in; she was very agitated and distressed and told him the Good Wife of Laggan had suddenly taken ill that day while out getting peats, and that she was near to death. 'Dear, dear', said her husband, 'I must come and see her then.' When he reached her house he found all the neighbours gathered round her. Striding over to the bed he stripped the clothes from her, revealing her terrible wounds and cried, 'See the object of your grief. This morning she assisted in the drowning of *Iain Garbh* (Rugged John) of Raasay' – an island between Skye and the Mainland – 'and today she tried to make me share his fate. But Providence has overtaken the servant of Satan and she is now about to die and suffer due punishment in the world to come.' It could not be denied from the state of the 'Good Wife's' injuries that the hunter was telling the truth; she offered no defence of herself. Instead, she told those gathered round her how she had become involved in witchcraft and confessed to her many crimes, including helping to drown the Raasay man that day. She then died a violent and painful death.

That night two men were travelling to Badenoch across the Monadhliath hills. When they were about half-way across the mountain they met a woman with blood pouring down the front of her body, running frantically towards Strathdearn (which they had just left), and screaming terribly. They had not gone on very far when they met two black dogs on the scent of something: and not far behind them came a black man riding on a black horse. He asked the travellers if they had seen a woman and they said they had, and that she had apparently been followed by two dogs. The man then asked them 'Would the dogs have caught her before she reached the churchyard at Dalarossie?' and the men replied that it was very probable. They went on, and just as they were coming out of the forest of Monadhliath, they were overtaken by the mysterious rider who had now the woman slung over his saddle, with the teeth of one dog fixed in her breast and the other fastened to her thigh. The men asked the rider where he overtook the woman: 'Just as she was going to enter Dalarossie Churchyard' he replied. It was only when the men got home that they heard of the fate of the Good Wife of Laggan; and it was recognised by all the community that her spirit was desperately trying to reach the churchyard at Dalarossie which was sacred ground, and so provided sanctuary to the living; but it was a singular place in that it also afforded protection to the souls of the dead from the Devil, provided they could reach its shelter before he could snatch them from its powerful precincts.

Pennant, writing in the eighteenth century about Banffshire says that 'some superstitions still lurk even in this cultivated country. The farmers carefully preserve their cattle against witchcraft by placing boughs of the mountain ash (rowan) and honeysuckle in their cow houses on 2 May. They hope to preserve the milk of their cows, and their wives from miscarriage by tying red threads about them'; the supposed witch was bled in order to make her confess to her evil practices. One of the great powers of witches was allegedly that of depriving people's cows of their milk by magic means. This was a widespread belief, and it could be performed in a number of different ways. The witch could put the Evil Eye on a beast, and cattle, rather than sheep, were believed to be more vulnerable in this respect. Pennant once more records some interesting information on this aspect of witchcraft:

If any good housewife perceives the effect of the malicious on any of her kine, she takes as much milk as she can drain from the enchanted herd, for the witch commonly leaves very little. She then boils it with certain herbs, and adds to them flints and untempered steel; after that she secures the door and invokes the three sacred persons. This puts the witch into such an agony, that she comes nilling-willing to the house, begs to be admitted to obtain relief by touching the powerful pot; the good woman then makes her terms: the witch restores the milk to the cattle, and in return is freed from her pains.

While on the subject of witchcraft and magic practices to do harm to others, it may be apposite to note another tradition in the same vein recorded by Pennant. He goes on to say that milk may be taken from cattle by means other than the Evil Eye and in order to determine this the following test is recommended: 'The tryal is made by immersing in milk a certain herb, and if the cows are supernaturally affected it instantly distills blood.' He then goes on to note magical revenge which an unsuccessful lover can work on his happy rival. The rejected lover '. . . takes three threads of different hues, and ties three knots on each, three times imprecating the most cruel disappointments on the nuptial bed: but the bridegroom to avert the harm, stands at the altar with an untied shoe and puts a sixpence beneath his foot.' The use of coloured threads in both black and white witchcraft was widespread in the Highlands, even until comparatively recent times, and much-believed in.

Shaw, writing in the late eighteenth century of customs in his part of the Highlands, records that witches and belief in their powers were commonplace and caused the church much alarm. Practices of this evil and pagan nature were in fact so prevalent in his day that every person over twelve years of age had to swear each year never to perform spells, enchantments or witchcraft of any kind. Witches were there, as elsewhere, believed to hold their meetings in churches and churchyards; they could turn themselves at will into mares, cats or hares. Their delight was to cause sickness and disease of every kind, raise storms at sea and drown their enemies, and turn the Evil Eye on whatsoever they envied or disliked. Martin Martin notes certain things about witches and others embued with evil or anti-social powers. In the islands in his day people believed that not only could the milk be taken from the cows by magic, but also from nursing mothers or wet-nurses. He himself saw four women whose milk was tested so that one might be chosen to act as nurse to a certain child. The woman with the best milk was selected but after three days her milk disappeared. As a result, she was dismissed from service and another woman chosen. The third day after that, the first nurse recovered her milk. It was locally concluded that the initial loss was brought about by the powers of witchcraft.

Other people were accredited with the power of taking away the substance of malt so that drink made of malt so enchanted had no strength and no taste. The charmer, however, who was responsible, then brewed particularly good and potent ale. Martin himself knew a man who was without a single drop of good ale in his house for a whole year; he was always complaining about this and finally a local wise man told him to obtain some yeast from every ale-house in the Parish. He got some from one particular man which he put amongst his wort and was able to make as good ale as could be found, and so the charm was defeated. Ale was, of course, the ancient drink of the Celts everywhere, and there are many stories told in the ancient and more recent tradition about it; according to the early Irish tradition it was the drink of the gods, the elixir dispensed to god and man alike at the Otherworld feast.

Martin likewise heard many examples of the belief in the powers of certain people to take away the milk from cows by the powers of witchcraft. Various kinds of charms were employed in order to bring this about. The flow of milk was transferred to the witches' own cows, or obtained in some other way; there is a large repertoire of very extraordinary tales told about this widely-held Highland belief. People held that milk, obtained by magic, did not produce the ordinary amount of butter; and also, that the curds of such milk were so tough and rubbery that they could not be made into good cheese; they were also unnaturally light in weight. It was held that butter taken away and mixed in with the charmer's own butter could be detected because the two were different in colour. The charmed butter was paler than the other; if a woman was found to have butter of this kind she was immediately deemed guilty of having performed this kind of witchcraft. The thing to do to remedy this state of affairs was to take a little rennet from the suspected charmer and place it in an egg-shell full of milk; unlike the ordinary blend of milk and rennet, the mixture would not curdle. Many people, even the most hardheaded, gave Martin examples of this and many claimed to have experienced such a loss themselves. Charms were used to prevent these powers, and many women put the root of groundsel amongst their cream as an amulet.

Many examples of witchcraft and belief in the powers of certain people have been recorded in the last century; it is not a subject that people care to talk about very much, but sympathetic and skilful collectors could, and still do, manage to obtain very interesting first-hand information on the subject. One remarkable instance was recorded by the great collector Father Allan MacDonald and published in his invaluable notebook of Hebridean traditions. A man, a Campbell, was on his way to Mass one Sunday morning at Kildonan. Walking along the strand, he came upon a woman and her daughter engaged in *a 'deilbh buidseachd,* 'framing spells', by crossing threads of various colours in a variety of ways in the same way as threads are arranged by weavers for the loom. He tore the structure to pieces and severely upraided the women for their evil, and especially for performing it on the Sabbath. They begged him not to speak of what he had seen and said if he kept quiet about it no harm should come to him. However, when Mass was over, he told all the people what he had seen. When he was about to sail to the mainland a crow perched on the mast, an evil omen, and as soon as the boat left the shore a terrible storm arose and he perished.

Witches could be encountered in human form, as in the episode above, but they could also be met with in the form of animals, the hare being the most common shape for metamorphosis. It was widely held that if arrows barbed with silver, or muskets loaded with a silver coin were pointed at them, or the metal struck them, the creature would immediately regain human form, and stand, often wounded, to reveal itself as a woman often known to, and respected by the one who had shot her. Another, very sinister aspect of witchcraft was the making of a clay or wax effigy of the person whom the witch desired to harm or destroy. Pins were stuck into this figure to the accompaniment of various incantations, and it was believed that the victim suffered agonising pain in the part into which the pin was inserted. Death could be caused by sticking a pin into the region of the heart. A recent instance of this was told to the writer: the image, which in this instance was not buried under the thatch of the victim's house, as was frequently the practice, but placed under a lonely waterfall, was made by a jealous lover whose girl had preferred another suitor. When he had deposited the fetish under the overhanging rock in a lonely glen on a small island in the Hebrides, he returned home. Shortly afterwards his rival became ill. He fell into a decline and caused concern to all his friends. As he grew daily worse, some local boys noticed that, every evening, the jealous lover made off for the moor alone. They wondered what he was up to and decided to follow him. When he reached the stream, they hid and observed what he did. They saw him take some object from behind the waterfall, bend over it, and then replace it and set off for the township again. When he had disappeared they went to the spot and found the clay image, stuck over with pins. They took out every pin, using the correct words, and then destroyed the *corp creadha,* 'clay body'. By the time they had returned home the sick man was already much improved, and his complete recovery was rapid thereafter.

There were many stories in circulation of these clay or wax images, and they were regarded as perhaps the most evil aspect of witchcraft. John Gregorson Campbell who collected many stories of witchcraft and the Black Arts in the Highlands in the last century, records a very good example of this widespread and much-feared practice. He regards it as typical of such stories. There was a notorious thief who came from Ardnamurchan. He stole so many cattle from the chief of the MacLeans of Dowart (Duart) that the landowner became his sworn enemy. On one occasion, he was passing the chapel and burial ground of Pennygown on the Sound of Mull. He noticed a light in the chapel and, on entering the building, he saw three witches sticking pins into a clay image which was intended to represent MacLean of Dowart. As each pin was venomously inserted, the chief was, as was later known, seized with an agonising pain in the part of his body selected by the witches. At last, only one pin remained and this was intended for his heart – the fatal stroke. MacIain sprang on the witches and put them to flight, seized the clay figure and hastened to the chief's house, where he found him on the point of death. He removed each pin in the presence of the sick man, and when the final pin was taken out, the MacLean got up, completely recovered. From that time on, he became the thief's most devoted friend.

Another very interesting story of this widespread and malicious practice was recorded in Perthshire, at Strathfillan. A minister there became afflicted with severe pains all over his body and fell into a wasting sickness. No doctor could discover the cause of his sickness. One morning, a woman from the far side of the river was on her way to call on the sick man and enquire after his health, when she observed another woman ahead of her and she knew she had a reputation in the locality for being a witch. Her suspicions were aroused, because it was still early morning, and she followed her. The alleged witch came to a hollow and there she buried something. The good woman dug this up when the other had gone and found it was a piece of wood stuck all over with pins. She at once took it to the Manse and revealed it, to the consternation of the witch, who was also visiting the sick man. As each pin was pulled out, the minister was instantly restored to health. It was also widely believed that no person lacking any limb could be affected by this evil form of magic; they must be completely whole in body.

Witches were believed to be capable of producing diseases in a variety of ways, apart from the use of the *corp creadha*. Campbell records how a young tailor, named Cumming, from Rannoch in Perthshire, fell into a wasting sickness. He told people that his terrible state was caused by witches who used to come to him at night and change him into a horse which they then proceeded to ride on through the air to Edinburgh and back. In the morning he was completely exhausted. The belief that witches turned men into horses for their own purposes and rode them until they were almost dead is widespread, and has many variants.

Witches were disliked and feared in the Highlands and Islands and many counter-charms were made as protection against them, but the actual persecution of them stopped long ago; the last witch to die in Scotland was burned at Dornoch in Sutherland in 1722 for having allegedly transformed her own daughter into a horse and having her shod by the Devil. A method of transforming people into other shapes was to shake a bridle at them; and in some areas, death could be brought about, according to local belief, by accompanying this action by an incantation. One of the means of getting the milk from someone else's cows was to 'milk' the *slabhraidh* or pot-chain (the chain which hung over the open fire and from which the great pot which boiled the water and cooked the food in every Highland home was suspended). Campbell records some extraordinary means whereby the stolen milk could be conveyed home by the witch. A native of Tiree took all the milk from the Laird of Coll's cows. She had it in a piece of black seaweed, wrapped round her body. A man met with her and, guessing what she had been up to, cut the seaweed with a knife; immediately, all the milk flowed forth. Witches were believed to be capable of carrying away milk in a number of different ways, some seemingly quite ridiculous, for example in needles, dung-forks and so on. The powers of witches must be counteracted by protective measures. Juniper had strong apotropaic qualities; it must be gathered in a certain way, burned before the cattle and then a sprig was placed in the animals tails as a charm against evil. In some instances a ball of hair – *ronag* – was put in the milk-pail on Lammas-day in order to keep the substance in the milk for the rest of the year.

Stale urine was another powerful antidote for the Evil Eye and other malignant spells, and rowan, as always, more powerful than any other wood. It was believed widely that the handle of the churn should be made of rowan wood. Only a few years before Campbell wrote his book on witchcraft he recorded that in Islay a man used to have a rowan tree collar with which he habitually tied up his cow at night; and every time the cow went to the bull, her owner passed the rowan collar three times through the chimney crook. On 1 May, Beltain, he decorated the whole house with sprigs of rowan. Campbell also notes an interesting tradition concerning a man from Craignish who habitually collected herbs with magic qualities on St Swithun's Day and studied the magical arts with one foot on the chimney crook. This is reminiscent of the Old Irish Druidic spells which used to be chanted while the enchanter went round a particular place or group of people on one foot. Stallions were proof against witches, and no person riding a stallion could be harmed by this dread power. If all charms failed, some of the enchanted cow's urine was placed in a well-corked bottle. The witch was then unable to pass water until she had restored the flow of milk to the beast. If pins were boiled in some of the milk of an afflicted cow until the vessel was dry, then the witch would appear and confess her guilt. In Skye it was apparently a custom to put the bull on top of the alleged witch's house; this was sure to bring back the milk to the cows. The tradition of drawing blood from a witch, although known, seems not to have been much in vogue in the Highlands. One plant, amongst many to which magical powers were attributed, was the pearlwort (*mothan*); when this was put into the milk-pail, the good would gradually return to the milk. A piece of it inserted into the bull's hoof at the time of mating, ensured the milk from the future calf would be immune from the powers of witchcraft.

Amongst their many dread and sinister powers that of raising

storms at sea and causing death and suffering to those who
navigated the treacherous waters of the Highland coasts was one of
the most deeply-feared by the Gaels. There are countless stories in
the west of terrible events brought about by these ruthless creatures.
The most famous witches in the western Islands for raising storms
were the Lewis witches. They were also able to get the fish from the
sea by magic. One episode, recorded by Campbell, tells how a Barra
witch contested with the other powerful witches of the islands, and
took the whole catch to Castlebay. One witch used to disappear in
human form from her home every night. This baffled her husband
who eventually decided to follow her. To his amazement, she turned
into a cat, and, in the name of the Devil, set out to sea in a sieve
with seven other cats. The horrified man called upon the Trinity,
and instantly the sieve upturned and the witches were drowned.
Egg-shells were used as boats by witches; for this reason one must
always pierce the bottom of an eggshell in order to prevent the
witches from using it for this purpose.

One way in which witches were alleged to sink vessels was to
place a *cuach,* a small round wooden dish, in a milk-pail full of
water. They would then begin certain incantations and the dish
would capsize; at that moment the ship would sink at sea. Some
years before Campbell wrote, a boat was lost between Raasay and
Skye. The witches responsible for this crime were seen at work near
a stream in the Braes of Portree. There were three of them, and, in
this instance, the presence of a man was also necessary. They floated
a cockle-shell in a pool and then arranged a number of black stones
round the edge of the pool. They began to recite an incantation, and

Witches' animals

when it reached its climax, the black stones began to bark like dogs; the cockle-shell disappeared and the ship sank.

There were male witches — magicians — as well as female, and certain of these achieved a widespread notoriety. It was believed that those who had practised the black arts in life were restless after death; they could cause a lot of trouble until they were safely buried. A Tiree tradition tells of a head-stone which had been placed at the grave of a man who had been supposed to be a master of the dark art; the stone would not remain in the same place, but was constantly found in a different position. Eventually it had to be secured at the head of the grave by a chain. One sure means of detecting a witch was as follows: early on the morning of the first Monday of each quarter, the smoke from the house of one who was a witch could be seen to 'go' against the wind. In this manner it was believed a witch could be identified.

Finally, the most famous witch story of the western Highlands concerns the hero MacGille Chaluim Ratharsaidh, Iain Mac Gille Chaluim of Raasay. He is a historical figure and the legend is widely believed to be true. He was drowned on 19 April 1671 on his way home from visiting the Earl of Seaforth in Lewis. Tradition holds that his death was due to the evil powers of his *muime* 'foster-mother', who enlisted the aid of several famous witches to raise a terrible storm in order to destroy him. Some of these were the renowned Yellow Foot from Skye, the Blue-Eyed from Skye, and Black Doideag from Mull. Iain's foster-mother lived on a small island to the north of Trotternish in Skye. No one knew what Iain had done to arouse her violent hatred in this way. He left Lewis on a clear, calm day. When his foster-mother, who was keeping watch on the sea from her island, saw his ship approaching, she placed a large vessel and a small vessel to float in the milk. She was a milk-maid on the island, and she set the calf-herd at the door of the shieling where he could see both 'Iain's ship and the two vessels floating in the milk. She herself stood by the fire, with one foot in the *slabhraidh* (pot-chain) again, and began incanting; immediately the little vessel began to be violently agitated. The boy then cried out that the small dish was going sunwise round the big dish; the violent motion then made it go widdershins (*tuathail* — anti-sunwise). It shook the side of the milk vessel, then turned upside down and floated, bottom up. At that very moment Iain's ship disappeared and the boy saw it no more. When the galley was halfway to the island off Trotternish, three ravens (the form taken on by the triple war goddess of ancient Ireland) were seen hovering about the boat in the wild storm that had developed so suddenly. Soon after this, 20 birds flew into the boat and took on the form of frogs. Then, all the witches of Scotland assembled round Iain's doomed ship. Even so, they were powerless to sink it until Iain cried 'What the Devil brought you here?' The naming of the Evil One sealed his fate. He became quite distracted by all the birds and the frogs. Eventually a huge raven landed on the gunwale beside him and he drew his sword to kill it, and in his rage and confusion he drove it right through the gunwale, where it stuck. Tradition varies as to what followed. Some say that Iain's ghost appeared before his widow and said:

> Friday came the wind
> And stirred itself to rage and fury;
> Tell thou the mother of my body
> That it was the evil ones that brought death.

The spirit allegedly repeated these lines three times. In 1861 a story-teller in Skye said that Iain's foster-mother drowned her charge in order to obtain money; as soon as she had succeeded in her evil ploy she is said to have bitterly regretted it.

Iain and his wife used to sail to Raasay alone together. On one occasion they were sailing to Harris and passing the coast of Trotternish when Iain fell out into the sea. The boat was moving at some speed and the sea was high. Iain's wife managed to seize her husband by the hair and hauled him aboard again with difficulty. The man who told this story also recited the lament traditionally sung by Iain's wife when the news of his tragedy reached her:

> As I sit on the beach
> Without joy or gladness,
> Never more shall I raise a blithe song
> After the Friday of my woe.
>
> The greyhounds are unstirring,
> Without tail-wagging or rejoicing,

Without welcome from the noble
Whose forebears were manly.

Without coursing or huntsmen,
Without trek to the hill,
To the heights of the hunt,
To the rough peaks of the Cuilinn.

These are some examples of the hundreds of stories of witches who, in days gone by, and even not so long ago, used to terrorise the simple peoples of the Highlands and the Islands of the west with their alleged powers of sinking ships, raising storms by means of threads and wooden bowls; who took the milk from people's cows, caused woe by their evil glance, and turned themselves into a variety of animals for the forwarding of their evil pursuits. And even today, although rarely spoken of, there are certain people living in remote areas who cause some misgiving in the minds of their neighbours whose belief in the old powers of evil are still not quite extinct.

Over and above straightforward witchcraft, many people were believed to have certain powers, sometimes extremely limited, which enabled them to work woe or well on their fellows.

Although the power of the *Droch Shùil*, 'Evil Eye', was usually attributed to witches and other persons of evil intent, it could be possessed by one who meant no ill and hated the gift. These people were quite unable not to blight things they admired. Over and above rowan branches, horseshoes and certain plants, some stones could assist in turning aside this unfortunate power. It could also be averted by drinking three mouthfuls of water which had been poured over silver (i.e. a silver coin); each mouthful must be taken in the name of the Trinity. The following incantation was sometimes made:

It is my own eye,
It is God's eye,
It is the eye of the Son of God
Which shall repel this,
Which shall combat this.

Certain river stones were believed to have magical properties and these could be used both as amulets against evil, or, in the case of black magic, as charms to promote harm. In one glen in central Perthshire, every house, including the church, has its gate-posts capped by a pair of fantastically shaped stones which have been worn into these weird forms by the action of the strongly-flowing river from which they have been taken. Local people will tell you that they are purely decorative, but one old man, well-versed in the traditional lore of the glen where he and his ancestors had always lived, informed the present writer that it was an ancient local belief that these strange stones from the nearby river had powers of keeping evil forces from the dwellings and the church. It was interesting to note that the War Memorial, high up the glen, which is conical in shape and composed of ordinary stones, is crowned by a very fine example of these singular, water-worn boulders.

River stones believed to be possessed of remarkable powers were often blackened in the fire, and incantations were made over them in order to bring harm to some unfortunate person who had incurred the hostility of the charmer. At the end of the last century, in the same area of central Perthshire, such a curse was carried out by means of a circle of blackened stones, the right state of the moon, and ritual chants; the victim did in fact die, although in normal health at the time. It became known to the local people what had been done, and by whom, and the man in question was evicted from his holding by the landlord or, as they put it locally, 'sent over the hill'. The writer had this information from an old man, a native of the place where the event happened, whose father had actually witnessed the incident; the spot where the circle of blackened stones was made is still known. The alleged magical properties of certain stones are further discussed on p. 92 ff. Some charms were incanted for specific types of evil magic, others to counteract enchantment in general. One of the latter, much used in the Outer Isles, is associated, like so many, with the beloved saint, Brigit or Bride, once a powerful goddess invoked widely over the pagan Celtic world and in Christian times venerated as Saint Brigit of Kildare where, in true pagan fashion, nine virgins perpetually attended her fire, which was never allowed to be extinguished.

Prehistoric stone monuments were inevitably regarded as the work of divine beings and forces, and were held in a superstitious reverance at variance with Christian tenets. The standing stones of Callanish, part tomb,

the site of ancestor worship; part observatory for solar and lunar phenomena; part water shrine, were understandably a focus of popular belief
and legend. The ceremonial 'avenue' was, even lately, used for communal
processions, especially on May Day and Midsummer's Day, times when
the powers of the stones were greatest. People spoke of 'going to the
stones' as a necessary ritual. M. Martin (1934) even referred to the site as
a 'Heathen Temple', and as such it was regarded by an anxious church.

A substance which was widely believed to be imbued with a
certain magic power in the Highlands was cheese. This was
regarded as a powerful protection against the danger of wandering
away from the correct track in the thick mists which come down so
suddenly in the wild mountainous country of the north and entirely
blot out the dangerous cliffs and bogs that form so great a hazard to
the traveller. Many wells are known as the Cheese Well, and it
seems likely that it was at one time a custom to make an offering of
cheese to a sacred well in some remote place, in order to obtain
protection from the understandable fear of becoming enshrouded in
one of these dread mists and meeting a miserable fate in barren and
treacherous countryside.

A charm used for the cure of sickness in man or beast was known
as *eòlas*, 'knowledge'. Hundreds of such charms have been collected
all over the Highlands and Islands; there is a strong Catholic
influence in these charms as the names of the saints invoked indicate,
especially St Brigit, St Columba, St Michael and St Peter. People
possessing the power of white witchcraft used to utter such charms
over the ailing creature, while performing the requisite ritual at the
same time. The *eòlas* or charm must also be repeated over water to
be drunk by or poured over a sick person or beast. When beasts
were sick, or human beings, as the case may be, those seeking a cure
for the sick would walk for miles in order to get a vessel of sacred
water over which some charmer had made an incantation. People
were not always willing to impart information about the words used
in healing or about the ritual involved; sometimes those cured were
sworn to secrecy as to how the healing was performed, and
complete silence throughout on the part of the sick person was a
frequent requisite. The writer has known charmers who would not
divulge their methods even to their husbands or wives. The Church,
as well as the medical profession, frowns on these practices; the
Church because they savour of paganism, the doctors because they

have no faith in them. But even doctors of high repute in the Highlands who have, themselves, been unable to cure a sick person, have expressed astonishment when a swift cure has been effected by a sincere charmer.

The *eòlas* was usually employed to cure illnesses of a limited kind such as toothache, bruises, urinary infections, swellings in the breast, epilepsy, and, very frequently, sprains, which were very common in rough, uneven country. The humblest of old women were often believed to have this power, and although any payment for a cure was prohibited, people often used to make some small present in kind for a bottle of special water and a healing charm. If the person going for a cure had to make a long journey he must take up lodgings for the night before sunset; in some localities it was believed to be preferable if no lodging was taken on that night, and no food eaten. There are many stories told of the healing powers of certain people, often in conjunction with some other sacred object or objects, such as stones, a holy well, a human skull and so on. One of the great curses of the Highlands and Islands is the high incidence of epilepsy, and many cures were tried in order to rid the afflicted person of the dread disease. One example of this which occurred in the parish of Nigg in the last century concerns a boy of 15 who was very ill with epileptic fits. His distressed relatives first tried to cure him with the charm of mole's blood. A plate was placed on the boy's head; the live mole was held over the plate by the tail, its head cut off, and the blood allowed to drop onto the plate. Three moles were sacrificed, one after the other, but with no result. Next they tried the effect of a piece of the skull of a suicide; in order to obtain this, a journey of well over sixty miles had to be made. When the piece of bone was acquired, it was scraped to dust and mixed into a cup of water. The boy was made to swallow this concoction without knowing what it was. The results were not recorded, but the information was given to the informant, a patient of the doctor who noted the incident, by the sister of the epileptic boy. The skull of a suicide, often filled with water from a holy well, was a known and much-believed-in cure for epilepsy, but it was held in reserve as a final measure when all other, less dramatic remedies had failed. In Lewis, the skull of an ancestor would be dug up from a special place in the graveyard, after sunset and before sunrise and water placed in it from a sacred well; this was then taken to the patient and he or she had to drink it, the whole ritual, from beginning to end, being performed in silence.

Because all matters of belief and superstitious practice are somewhat delicate, and information is often imparted in confidence it has been decided by the writer not to give details of names or exact localities where first-hand information on ancient and often non-Christian practices has been obtained, and ritual actually witnessed. The most remarkable example of a human skull being used in the cure of epilepsy, with, seemingly, unfailing success was told to the writer by the guardian of the skull, the man who actually performed the cures. A holy well, on a remote hillside, was an essential part of the procedure, and the well was called *Tobar a' Chinn*, 'The Well of the Head'. The story is as follows. In an isolated township in Wester Ross, in some of the wildest and most beautiful country in the entire Highlands, some 200 years ago a local woman committed suicide. According to religious custom, no suicide could be buried in the churchyard; her body was thus interred on the moor, outside the sacred precincts. After a short time, her skull suddenly appeared miraculously, lying on the surface of the ground. According to the guardian, the 'wise men' of the township recognised this as a sign that it was to be used as a cure for epilepsy, for the crania of suicides were believed to have more potent powers of healing than those of people who had died in any other way. The waters of the well higher up on the hill were believed to have certain healing powers, and it was a powerful and ancient Celtic belief, of which there are many examples, that by placing a human head in a venerated well, the powers of the water — whatever they were, healing in general, effecting specific cures, imparting fertility, and so on — were markedly increased by the magic powers with which the human head was accredited in the Celtic world down the centuries. The skull was taken to the well and kept in a small stone coffin-like container, where it still lies. The guardian, a local charmer, was appointed and the position has remained hereditary to this day; cures are still performed on occasion. The well is not supposed to be visited for any purpose other than the healing of epileptics, for it is locally believed that the powers of the water are not inexhaustible, and must be used with care. The writer was in fact taken to see the well and the head, and the ritual was explained in detail by the guardian himself. The well lies in a hollow in the hill, and it would be virtually impossible to chance upon it.

The fame of the cure was apparently so great in the western Highlands and Islands that people who were seemingly incurable would travel there from great distances in the belief that it would not fail to bring relief from this deeply-distressing affliction. The patient and his (or her) companions must go to the house of the guardian. There, they would be instructed in the correct ritual; violation of any aspect of it would be certain to ruin all chances of a cure. The patient must climb the hill alone with the guardian. The ceremony had to be carried out after the sun had left the hill, and before it reached it again. Complete silence must be observed both on the long climb up to the well, and on the return to the house. Once the well was reached, the guardian took the skull from its box and approached the well; the patient had to walk three times sunwise round the well (*deiseal*). The guardian then dipped the skull in the water and gave it to the suffering person in the name of the Trinity; this he did three times. He then put the 'prohibitions' on the patient, things that he must never do. What these were were not divulged. Then the descent back to the house was made. Before leaving for the hill, the guardian asks the patient if he has complete faith in the power of the healing water. If there is any hesitation whatsoever about this, then he is not treated. It is widely believed all over the west that there has never been one failure to effect the cure. Although modern medical treatment for the control of epilepsy has lessened the popularity of this archaic folk healing, some people still prefer it, so great is their faith in its efficacy.

Various other methods for curing the widespread disease of epilepsy, which did not necessarily involve a charmer, were resorted to in different parts of the Highlands. Sacrifice of different kinds could be made. For example, it was believed that if a hen or a cock, a drake or a gander were buried alive at the exact spot where the epileptic had his or her first falling fit, no second attack would ever occur. Carmichael records an account of this given to him by a Ross-shire woman. A boy whose sister had an epileptic fit came to her mother to get a black cock which he knew she had. The bird was immediately buried alive at the spot where the girl had fallen. The girl was then a middle-aged woman, but she never had another attack of epilepsy. Again, in Ross-shire, in the last century a minister records how he talked to his mother-in-law about the burying alive of a black cock at Evanton for the same purpose. She told him she had seen the girl in question fall in a fit on the floor of an upper room in the house. Straight away a hole was made at the spot where the girl fell, and a second hole made through the lower floor into the earth. A black cock was then procured, lowered down through the two floors and buried alive in the hole. Carmichael also records that some years previous to his writing, a boat was crossing Loch Duthaich from Letterfearn to Dornie, when a man in the boat had an epileptic fit. The other men took bearings, turned back to the shore, and obtained a black cock which they put, together with a stone, in a sack. When they reached the point where their companion had had his fit, they threw the sack with its victim into the water. The man, allegedly, never had another epileptic fit. Sometimes the blood of a black cock was sprinkled over one who was afflicted by the falling sickness; if no black cock was available, the blood of a black cat was used instead.

Among their numerous alleged powers, witches were accredited with the ability to delay the birth of a child. This was brought about by means of a ball of black thread which was kept in a black bag at the base of the witch's weaving loom, where it could not be seen. If the ball of thread was found and removed, then the power of the witch was destroyed. One story told in the Highlands has it that a child was kept in its mother's womb for 22 years by means of witchcraft. When it was born, it had hair, teeth and a beard. This unlikely legend seems to hark back to early Celtic mythological tales in which a supernatural woman gives birth to a child who is already a mature and fully-armed warrior! One tale of this kind, related by Campbell concerns the mother of a well-known Highland character, *Ailein nan Sop* (Allan of the Straws). She was a servant, who was made pregnant by a married man. The wife learnt of this, was duly enraged, and went to a local witch for help. The witch gave her a certain bone, and told her that as long as the bone was kept, the birth of the child would be prevented. Allan remained in his mother's womb for fifteen months beyond the normal period of her pregnancy. When the husband, who had fathered the child, came to realise that his wife was responsible for this unnatural delay in the birth, he decided to outwit her. He arranged that his jester should come home one day, apparently very drunk, and smashing things around him as he made his unsteady way through the house. When he was reprimanded for this, he was to say that he had been in a house where a long overdue child had been born. The wife, on hearing this, thought that the witch had failed in her powers and in fury, seized the bone and threw it into the fire. It disappeared in a cloud of blue smoke; Allan was then born at once, with a full set of teeth! This is a widespread motif, having several different versions.

A great variety of amulets could be used to keep the dread powers of witchcraft at bay. Martin records that in Harris a species of nuts called Molluka were to be found; some of these were used as charms against the Evil Eye or witchcraft in general, the most efficacious being the white variety. They were placed about the necks of children to protect them; one of their great virtues was that if any evil was being planned against the wearer, the white nut would turn black. Martin attests to the truth of this, although he is unable to offer any rational explanation for it. The Steward of Harris, one Malcolm Campbell, told Martin that some weeks before his arrival there, all his cows gave blood instead of milk for several days. A wise neighbour told his wife that this was caused by witchcraft, and that the spell could be removed without undue difficulty. She was advised to take one of the white nuts and put it in the bottom of the pail into which she was about to milk the cows – this species of nut was known as the Virgin Mary's Nut. She did as she was told; the first cow to be milked gave nothing but blood, as before, but the nut turned dark brown. She used the nut again, and from that moment, all the cows gave pure milk.

Belonging as it does to the category of folk belief connected with witchcraft, good and bad, the widespread belief in the power of certain people, voluntarily or involuntarily, to inflict woe on others by means of a glance of their eye, is one of the most rich and interesting aspects of Highland folklore. Carmichael collected a huge body of lore about the Evil Eye, and recorded many fascinating methods and incantations whereby its powers may be overcome:

> Four to work sickness with Evil Eye,
> Man and woman, youth and maid;
> Three to repel ill will,
> Father and Son and Holy Spirit.

Deeply-rooted and ancient traditions underlie the widespread belief in this evil power; it filled people with dread, and many people feared it so much that their whole lives were hemmed in and affected by tabu connected with it. One rhyme must be said on the first Monday of the quarter, a dangerous day:

> The first Monday of the quarter,
> Take care that luck leave not thy dwelling.
>
> The first Monday of the Spring quarter,
> Leave not thy cattle neglected.

According to Carmichael, some men observed this injunction so closely that they kept their beasts indoors all day on those ominous occasions, only letting them out at nightfall, lest the Evil Eye should fall on them. Only the eye of their owner was permitted to rest on them.

There were many antidotes for this form of witchcraft, and Carmichael was told an interesting tale of this by a man who was a stone-mason. One spring, his father was busy with the ploughing when a man from the other side of the loch came across to see if he could get some oat seed. He was given this, and went home the way that he had come. He was very grateful for the favour that he had received. On the instant that he turned away, the man's mare apparently fell down dead. The mason's father ran into the house shouting that the man to whom he had been so generous had put the 'Eye' on his horse. The man was then followed so that he could repair the serious damage he had caused. The offender was one of the unfortunates who could not prevent his power, and he was extremely distressed about the occurrence. He explained his powerlessness over his unfortunate faculty. He then went three times sunwise round the mare, singing a rune of aiding and praying to the Trinity to undo the damage that the eye had done to the animal. As soon as he had finished this ritual, the mare lifted her head and rose up alive and fit. The man with the 'Eye' said again how the episode had distressed him, but that he had no means of averting it.

There are innumerable fascinating charms for the Evil Eye in the Highlands. According to one woman, a native of Bonar Bridge, in

order to counteract the 'Eye' one must rise early in the morning and
go to a boundary stream over which the living and the dead have
passed – a very magical point. One must then lift a small palmful of
water from the lower side of the bridge, in the name of the Trinity.
Next one must retrace one's steps with the palmful of water in a
wooden bowl, and sprinkle the sacred liquid on the backbone of the
animal on which the Evil Eye has rested. All must be performed in
the name of Christianity. Next the water in the bowl must be
sprinkled behind the fire-flag again in the name of the Trinity.
According to this informant, to follow the procedure closely would
be certain to bring about complete healing in the stricken animal,
and destroy the force of the Evil Eye:

> Thy strait be on the fire-flags,
> Thine ailment on the wicked woman.

A moving incantation, a splendid blend of pagan magic and
Christian faith was collected by Carmichael in the island of Barra.
Three mouthfuls of water in which a silver coin had been placed
must be drunk by the victim, the first mouthful in the name of the
Father, the second in the name of the Son, and the third in the name
of the Spirit:

> It is mine own eye,
> It is the eye of God,
> It is the eye of God's Son,
> Which shall repel this,
> Which shall combat this.
>
> He who has made to thee the eye,
> Surely lie it on himself,
> Surely lie it on his affection,
> Surely lie it on his stock.
>
> On his wife, on his children,
> On his means, on his dear ones,
> On his cattle, on his seed,
> And on his comely kine.
>
> On his mares, grey and brown,
> On his geldings in the plough,

On his flocks black and white,
On his corn-barns, on his coarse meal.

On the little fairy women
Who are reeling in the knoll,
Who are biding in the heath,
Who are filling the cavities.

Another means of countering the power of the Evil Eye was recorded by Carmichael at Kiltarlity, Inverness-shire. One must take a clay vessel and go, once again, to running water, over which both the living and the dead cross. On the lower side of the bridge where this happened, one must go down on the right knee, lift a palmful of water in the hollows of the hands and put it in the dish, repeating the following words:

I am lifting a little drop of water
In the holy name of the Father;
I am lifting a little drop of water
In the holy name of the Spirit.

One must then rub a little of the sacred water into the two ears of the person, or on the part afflicted by the 'Eye', and down the spine of the afflicted animal saying:

Shake from thee thy harm,
Shake from thee thy jealousy,
Shake from thee thine illness,
In name of Father,
In name of Son,
In name of Holy Spirit.

The remainder of the water must then be poured on a grey stone or a fixed rock, so that its holy powers should not be abused. The name of the person or of the animal must be mentioned at the same time as the healing water is being applied.

Threads were used both to enchant and to remove enchantment in the Highlands, as well as to cure certain maladies, and this persisted well into living memory. The charm of the threads was made to sick animals, generally cattle. The threads in question were made into a cord of three ply and of three colours. This was symbolic of the Trinity — black, symbolic of the condemnation of God; red, symbolic of the Crucifixion; white, symbolising the purification of the spirit. The cord was twisted three times round the tail of the animal which had been bewitched, and it was then tied in a very complex, triple loop. Carmichael records how in February 1906 a Benbecula man came across to North Uist in order to buy a horse. Observing a fine animal outside the house of a certain crofter, he praised the beast and continued on his way. He had hardly passed out of sight when the horse had fallen to the ground and was rolling in agony. People knew this Benbecula man was reputed to have the 'Eye', so the owner of the horse immediately went to a woman versed in counteracting this distressing power. She twined with her teeth three threads of three ply, and different colours, and instructed the owner of the animal to tie these, one after the other, round the base of the horse's tail, in the name of the Trinity. He did as the woman advised, and at once the animal recovered. The charmer told the horse's owner that she had inherited this knowledge and power from her father, a very devout Christian, much given to prayer. She apparently was able to ascertain from the beginning of her prayer whether the illness had been brought about by natural sickness or by the Evil Eye. If the sickness was natural, then she would advocate conventional cures; if due to witchcraft, then she brought about the remedy by the power of her prayer. She maintained that the Evil Eye of a man, although less venomous than that of a woman, was more difficult to counteract then that of a woman. A common effect of their powers on all true charmers or healers, is the illness and weakness that they themselves experience after having performed their cure, sometimes almost to the point of death. To remove the damage brought about by witchcraft involved a severe struggle against the powers of evil and inevitably resulted in total mental and physical exhaustion. Such white witches, or charmers believed that their power came from God and that it was incumbant upon them to use it, no matter how unpleasant the consequences to themselves may be. Not to use the gift would involve its weakening and ultimate loss.

An interesting incantation appears in the Records of the Presbytery of Kintyre and Islay, dated November 1697. A

Malcolm MacMillan confessed he had practised a charm with a string, and some words he spoke over the string were entered into the Records in Gaelic. He used the string for the cure of rickets, demonic possession, other sudden distempers; he put the thread to his breath and said into it:

> I place the protection of God about thee,
> Mayest thou be shielded from every peril,
> May the Gospel of the God of grace
> Be from thy crown to the ground about thee.
> May men love thee
> And women not work thee harm.

When cattle were being sent to pasture, or returning home from it, the person in charge of them would leave one or two beasts to follow behind, in the belief that this will ward off the Evil Eye, which allegedly required the whole stock to be in front of the herd.

One very moving story about belief in the power of the 'Eye' and deep faith in the ability of white witches to undo the results is told of a little boy from Leitir, Loch Duthaich, who had the misfortune to have the 'Eye' put on him. The child became desperately sick and the parents were in despair; all conventional remedies failed. Finally the distracted father was advised to make the long journey to the head of Loch Carron where there was a woman famed for her powers of counteracting the fierce force of the Evil Eye. All he was required to do was to take some small piece of the boy's clothing with him. The charmer took the piece of cloth, went away, and performed some secret rites. She then told the man to return home where he would find his little son fit and well. This he did, and was amazed to find the child sitting on his mother's knee, lively and completely restored to health. But this particular cure took heavy toll of the charmer; the virtue had entirely left her, and for a day and a night she hung between life and death; she said she was always very ill after performing a counter-spell, whether it be for man or beast:

Charm for thwarting the 'Eye':

> Twelve eyes against every malice,
> Twelve eyes against every envy

Twelve eyes against every purpose
Twelve eyes against every hope
Twelve eyes against every intent,
Twelve eyes against every eye,
The twelve eyes of the Son of the God of life,
The twelve eyes of the Son of the God of life.

The writer has heard many traditions of the above kind, still extant amongst the old people in the Highlands and Islands, but there is understandably a deep reticence to talk about such things, and any detailed information known is usually imparted in strictest confidence. In central Perthshire there are still lingering memories about working the Evil Eye by means of sticks, the willow being used for this purpose; it was not possible to get an exact account of how this was done, but the counter-charm was performed by means of rowan. The whole process, however, was regarded as a close secret.

Belief in the power of the Evil Eye then, is extremely potent and widespread in the Scottish Highlands, and has a long ancestry in the Celtic world. One of the earliest Irish tales, the magnificent mythological story of the war between the gods of Ireland, 'The Second Battle of Moytura', concerns the malevolent god Balor Beumshuileach, 'Balor of the Evil Eye'. The eye was kept permanently closed, so great was its power of destruction when unlidded; when Balor's men were hard-pressed in battle, it took several men to lift the lid with sticks. The eye then sent out such potent rays of evil magic, that the entire opposing forces could be wiped out at one glance.

In the Inner Hebrides the charm for curing the Evil Eye must allegedly be made on a Thursday or a Sunday; in different places, different rhymes were used. Campbell, in his *Witchcraft,* recounts how an Islay woman achieved miraculous cures for the 'Eye' by using the following rhyme, which he publishes rather unwillingly, as such things were not easily divulged to strangers — or indeed, at all. In this case, an ancient charm had been transformed into a Christian prayer, which, as we have seen, must so often have been the case:

If eye has blighted,
Three have blessed,

Stronger are the Three that blessed,
Than the eye that blighted;
The Father, Son and Holy Ghost;
If anything elfin or worldly has harmed it,
On earth above,
Or in hell beneath,
Do, Thou, God of Grace, turn it aside.

This rhyme had to be repeated three times, in good Celtic fashion.

Guisers

---5---

Cures, Omens, Tabus and Social Customs

OVER AND above the repertoire of cures brought about by the prayers and skills of the charmers or white witches, there were many other folk cures in circulation in the Highlands, as elsewhere, both for people and for animals, some based on respectable herbal remedies, and others relying on magic of some kind. As long ago as the second century AD the writer Pliny noted some of the plants that were used by the Gauls for purposes of healing and protection and recorded the various ways in which they must be collected in order to make them magically efficacious. Martin Martin gives a long list of diseases known, and not known, in Skye and the smaller Isles. He too notes that ordinary remedies used by the natives were effected by plants, roots, stones, parts of animals, and so on. Blood-letting was widely practised. He tells of a smith in the parish of Kilmartin in Skye who was believed to be able to cure faintness of the spirits (Martin does not say exactly what disease this is). The patient was seemingly laid on the anvil with his face upwards; the smith then seized a large hammer in both his hands, and with a fierce expression approached the sick person. He then raised the hammer from the ground as if preparing to strike the patient with all his considerable strength. It was a risky cure to perform, because the smith must terrify the sick person, but use the hammer with so much skill that he did not in fact harm him. The smith in question was apparently famed for his pedigree; he constituted the thirteenth generation of smiths, all possessed of this healing power. This too represents an archaic Celtic belief. The smith not only held an elevated position in society; his power to handle the most potent charm against evil — iron — imbued him with semi-sacred powers in the eyes of his fellows, and many of the early Celtic smiths were believed to possess healing powers. It is an impressive feature of extant, or very recently extant Highland folklore, that one can constantly glimpse, beneath all the borrowings and accretions that have taken place down the centuries, traces of that much older, much more powerful Celtic world, where the gods and goddesses walked side by side with mankind, with goodwill or hostility, as the case might be, and where the day to day life of the people was moulded and controlled by hidden forces, the powers of which remain today as pale shadows.

It was a widespread belief that the seventh son of a seventh son had the ability to heal people of King's Evil (Scrofula). People with the power of healing were not always regarded with approval, especially by the Church; one famous physician, Neil Beaton of Skye, doctor to MacLeod of Dunvegan, was so skilled that it was darkly hinted by many that he had learnt his art from the Devil himself. He was in great demand all over the Highlands and Islands.

Together with cures for sickness induced by natural or magical agents, we must consider measures that could be taken to ward off ill-fortune before it had occurred. These include the reading of omens which could warn people of impending ill-luck, and things that must — or must not — be done in order to prevent evil powers from approaching in the first instance. In early Irish society, a hero, when he was first initiated into the elevated status of warrior, had a number of tabus, or *geasa* as they were called, placed on him. Violation of these tabus meant certain destruction. It was always the aim of enemies, whether natural or supernatural, to trick the hero into violating his tabus, and many of the tales are concerned with

the ways this was brought about. Tabu was also a major feature of
Highland folk-life, and there were lucky and unlucky days, times, or
situations, when things were or were not to be attempted. For
example, Martin again records that it was a custom of the natives
of Colonsay, after they had landed on Oronsay Isle, to make a tour
sunwise of the Church before they entered on any kind of business.
The ritual of going sunwise, often three times, round a church, a
holy well or a domestic building was very widespread indeed; it is
known in Gaelic as *deiseal*. It was a custom known to Martin, but
not openly practised in his day, in the island of Lewis, to make a
fiery circle about the houses, cattle, corn, and other possessions
belonging to every family. A man would carry the burning brand in
his right hand and move round in a sunwise direction. This
apotropaic round was performed in the village of Shadir in 1700,
but Martin records that it proved fatal to one man; he was called
MacCallum. The night after he had performed this undoubtedly
pagan rite, all his own property and possessions were destroyed by
fire.

The numbers and varieties of cures for various ills and the means
of averting ill-fortune are incredible. A great deal of superstition
attended the birth of a child, a time when both the mother and the
new-born infant were particularly vulnerable to all the forces of evil,
witchcraft, and fairy power. Once the child had been born, the
mother must on no account leave the house until she had been
kirked; unbaptised infants, like suicides, could not be buried in
sanctified ground. Often, when one is walking in a Highland
township with a native of the area, a small stone is pointed out
which marks the pathetic grave of some unfortunate babe who did
not survive long enough to find a place within the protective walls
of the churchyard. Iron was always regarded as a highly apotropaic
substance, and it was customary to place the iron tongs across the
cradle of an infant, especially if it was placed out of doors, in case
the fairies took it and substituted the healthy human baby for one of
their own sickly offspring. It was unlucky to rock an empty cradle if
one did not desire an increase in the family — to do so ensured that a
new baby would soon occupy it.

Ill omens were of many kinds, and could cause deep unease in
people. It was considered unlucky if a stray swarm of bees were to
settle on someone's property without being claimed by their owner.

It was, and still is, particularly unfortunate to catch sight of the new moon through glass; it should be seen out of doors, and various rites must be performed according to differing local tradition; it must be bowed to three times, or one must turn one's money over three times in one's pocket, and so on. To see the old moon in the arms of the new was a sign of good weather; the horns of the new moon must also be turned up – if they were turned down the water they retained would fall and flood the earth. McGregor records that in Soay, a small island off the south of Skye, when the head of the family died, a large lock of his hair was cut off and nailed firmly to the lintel of the door in order to keep away the fairies. There were various ways in which it was believed a snake-bite could be cured; the head of a serpent was preserved for years and rubbed onto the wound. This was believed to be an infallible cure. The dried head was placed in water and then the wound washed with it. It was also widely believed that only a charmer or white witch must set broken or otherwise damaged bones; qualified doctors were believed to know nothing of such matters. Another widespread belief was that it was unlucky to enter a house by the back door; the prospective occupier must always go in by the front entrance. There were many other strange cures for miscellaneous ills which were absolutely infallible in the eyes of the people; warts were common, but could be removed by washing them in rain water or in the blood of a pig. By putting gold rings in the ears, sore eyes could be healed; or the eye itself could be rubbed with some gold object while an incantation of healing was repeated. Other very general cures were the use of fried mice as a remedy for smallpox; a spider, sealed into a goose quill could relieve a child of the troublesome disease of thrush.

Much superstition and tabu was observed by sailors: certain things must not be given their correct name at sea – even places came into this custom. For example, Martin records that the natives of Canna called the island Tarsin when they were at sea. Certain birds were much feared at sea, as well as on land. The stormy petrel was regarded as a bad omen when it fluttered about the boats; a raven landing on the mast was a sure indication of witchcraft. In order to protect the vessel and those who sailed in her from the evil powers of fairies, witches, petrels, the Evil Eye and so on, a horseshoe was nailed onto the mast of the vessel – always a highly apotropaic object. Tabu then, both positive and negative, was widespread in the Highlands, and much lingers on, just as it does in other parts of the British Isles. It was considered to be highly unlucky if a stranger were to count one's children, cattle or sheep. And, if one were questioned as to numbers of any of these, one must always end by saying 'bless them'. An odd number should not sit at table, and especially thirteen. It was believed that the first person of such a number who rose from the table would die within the year. A stranger must never walk across a pile of fishing rods lying on the beach, or over ropes, oars or any other item of marine equipment. If he inadvertently did so, he must be made to retrace his steps so as to undo the potential ill-luck he had caused. People must only be served at table from left to right. This is another example of *deiseal* (p. 94 above); it was likewise considered to be unlucky in beginning to row a boat, or start a funeral or wedding procession except towards the right hand. To see a foal or a snail or to hear a cuckoo before having broken one's fast in the morning were also omens that the day would not go well:

> With its back to me turn'd I beheld the young foal,
> And the snail on the bare flag in motion so slow;
> Without tasting of food, lo, the cuckoo I heard,
> Then judged the year would not prosperously go.

A peculiar superstition was that it was unlucky to stand between an epileptic man and fire or water. Water should not be thrown out of a house after sunset and before sunrise. One must never dig a grave on Sunday as another would be sure to have to be dug during the week for another member of the family. It was important that a corpse should stiffen up after death, otherwise another member of the same family would die before the year was out. Other widespread and common beliefs include the tradition that the howling of a dog at night presaged death, as did the alighting on the roof of a house of a magpie or a crow. It was also regarded as being extremely unlucky to weigh new-born infants; this would certainly bring about their death. No cat must be allowed to sleep beside an infant as it would suck its breath and so kill it.

Martin records many tabus and cures current in his time. He says that the inhabitants of the Flannan Islands must never call St Kilda by its proper name, Hirt, but only 'the High Country'. Moreover, if they were fowling in the Flannan Islands, a common pursuit, they must not use the name Flannan, but 'the Country'. Other things must not be called by their proper name; *uisge*, Gaelic for water, must be called '*burn*'. A rock, *creag*, must be referred to as *cruaidh*, 'hard'. The Gaelic word for shore is *claddach* but the Flannan islanders must refer to it as *uamh*, 'cave'. 'Sour' in Gaelic is *gort*, but they had to use the word *gaire*. There are countless examples of such tabu words, sometimes the tabu being permanent, sometimes applying only to some particular situation or occasion. They must not kill a fowl after evening prayers had been said. No one might take away to his home any sheep-suet, no matter how many sheep were killed in the islands. Nothing must be stolen, unknown to one's partner; if food were taken in this way, serious sickness was bound to ensue. Martin, in his invaluable work, records an interesting superstition which he got, not only from natives of Lewis, but also from two people who had been in the Flannan Isles the previous year. Martin asked one of them if he prayed at home as fervently and as often as he did in the Flannan Isles and he confessed that he did not. He said that these remote islands were places of inherent sanctity; anyone landing there would find himself much more given to devotion there than anywhere else. The ancient classical writers refer to certain islands off the coast of Britain that were held in deep superstitious awe by the natives, and even today the Flannan Isles connote something mysterious and savouring of the Otherworld — the island home of the departed spirits, far in the western ocean. The Highlanders have always regarded certain days and certain seasons of the year as being particularly lucky or unlucky; this superstition likewise goes right back to the ancient Celtic world, when omens were read in order to determine whether a day was likely to be favourable or unfavourable to some activity or decision. The 14th of May was widely held to be an unlucky day, and indeed the whole week in which 14 May fell was looked upon as being inauspicious. May and January were not favoured months; Friday was always an unlucky day for a wedding. Alexander Carmichael collected many incantations connected with calendar superstitions. Some of these are given in sections connected with other, specific traditions (p. 117 ff).

Fire was, as always, an essential element in evil-averting rites; as we have seen, to carry a burning brand *deiseal* (sunwise) round a house was believed to purify and protect it. This was also performed in connection with women before they were churched after childbirth; fire was also carried sunwise about children before they were baptized; the ritual was performed both in the morning and the evening. It persisted at least into Martin's time, but he remarks that it was only performed by old midwives; as he deeply disapproved of this pagan custom, people may have been unwilling to be quite frank about this deep-rooted and ancient custom. When he showed his scorn of it, and asked why it was performed, the people were seemingly much annoyed by his attitude and refused to answer him. One or two, however, told him that the fire-round was a powerful means of preserving the mother and child from the ever-present forces of evil sprites, always seeking to do harm to mankind, and to snatch away the unguarded infant. The fairies were notoriously dangerous in this respect; once they could steal a healthy human babe, they would replace it by a puny, skeletal child which did not thrive, but had a voracious appetite; it would eat up everything that came its way and yet remain gaunt and under-nourished. It was customary for people in Martin's day, who believed that their babies had been abducted by the fairies, to dig a grave in the fields on Quarter-day (an important calendar day) and to put the changeling there overnight. In the morning they expected to go and find their own healthy child lying there in place of the fairy baby. There are many versions of the changeling legend. In Martin's time, some people used to perform these rounds sunwise about welcome strangers or people who had done them some good turn; they went round them three times, blessed them, and wished them success in all their affairs. This custom was likewise by no means kindly looked upon by the ministers of the Church.

Another ancient and widely-used antidote for plague or murrain in cattle and people was the process known as making *tein-éigin*, 'need-fire'. It was performed as follows: all the fires in the parish must be extinguished and then, according to Martin's account, it was necessary for 81 married men to participate in order to make the ritual successful. Two great planks of wood were taken and nine men were employed in turn to rub the two planks together until the great heat generated eventually produced fire. From this 'need' or 'forced' fire, every family must make a new fire in his home; as soon as this was blazing well, a cauldron of water was placed on it, and this sacred liquid was then sprinkled over people or beasts infected with the plague. The people swore in the efficacy of this practice, and, like so many Highland customs, its origins clearly belong to the distant past, with profound pagan associations connected with the magic of fire ritual in general. Martin records that it was practised on the mainland, opposite the south of Skye, within 30 years of his writing — and when such deeply-rooted customs finally ceased to be carried out in remote glens and islands is still open to question.

In the nineteenth century, Carmichael, in his invaluable collection of the ancient lore of Gaelic Scotland, gives posterity many further examples of portenteous signs, and the ways in which they may be interpreted. Lucky signs were known as *rathadach*; unlucky omens were called *rosadach*. Carmichael notes that the sight of a man, especially one with brown hair, is a good omen; a man coming towards or looking at the seer is likewise an excellent sign. But a man going away from the augurer is an extremely unfavourable omen. If a man is seen by the seer, standing, or an animal in the act of getting up, this means that a sick person is throwing off the disease. The reverse is indicative that the illness will continue. The sight of a woman is likewise regarded as fortunate, provided she does not have red hair; this is never lucky, any more than is left-handedness. *Corrach* means 'left-handed'; it also means tricky, crooked, and, in fact, in its true sense, sinister. There is some confusion in this vast repertoire of lucky and unlucky omens; according to some, for a seer to observe a woman standing is a sign of good luck; in the opinion of others, the reverse is the case. If the seer observes a woman approaching he should cross himself. It is also a bad omen if a woman is seen to be going away; a woman with light red hair is a bad omen; a woman with dark red hair is even worse. An augurer, performing an augury, must quickly cross himself if he sees a woman with red hair.

Sacrifices of various kinds were, as we have seen, performed for various purposes and for certain calendar festivals. Dark hints of human sacrifice underlie many of these vestigial pagan feasts; and human sacrifice, sometimes on a grand scale, was very much a feature of universal pre-Christian Celtic practice. There are also traces of its persistence into a Christian milieu, and even today, the saying *'Chaidh ùir air sùil Odhrain'*, 'Earth went over Odhran's eye', is widely heard in the Highlands and Islands, and people will

Iona

readily explain the meaning of this statement. When Saint Columba, best-loved of all the Celtic saints, left Ireland in the sixth century, in order to go into permanent exile, virtually as an act of martyrdom, he chose the island of Iona, because it was impossible to see Ireland from it; it is also possible that it was a Druidic sanctuary which he proceeded to Christianize. A legend, of a widespread kind, is told concerning the saint's efforts to erect the first building of his monastic community. No matter how soundly they were constructed, the walls, by the machinations of some evil spirit, collapsed as soon as they had been erected. Columba recognised that some propitiation was necessary and, on prayer, was told that the building would never remain standing unless a human foundation sacrifice was buried there alive. Lots were cast and Odhran was chosen; other versions of the legend say that he himself volunteered to be the victim. He was buried alive, and after three days, Columba was overcome with curiosity to find out how his follower fared, and ordered that he should be dug up. Odhran allegedly looked at the saint and said: 'There is no wonder in death, and hell is not as it is reported.' The saint was horrified by this unChristian statement and had Odhran buried again with all haste. Another version of the saying is *'Ùir! Ùir! air beul Odhrain'* 'Earth, earth, on Odhran's mouth'. Some people who still know the legend say that the story was invented by Columba's Druidic rivals in order to discredit the saint. Martin records that in his day it was traditional belief that Columba allowed no woman who was not a nun to stay on the island. Nearby is a small isle where all the tradesmen employed on the island had to keep their womenfolk, and for this reason it was known as the Island of Women. This seems to be an echo of the ancient pagan legend of small sacred islands which were entirely inhabited by women who were completely dedicated to the cult of some powerful deity; their rites often included human sacrifice, and no man must set foot on these islands. The women periodically left them in order to have intercourse with men; it is probable that the male issue of such unions were sacrificed, while the females were reared to become future initiates in the cult. The classical writers refer to such places, and there are references to them in the early Irish tales.

Things to do and things not to do encompass a large sphere of Highland life, for not only was daily life closely circumscribed by tabu and superstition; social intercourse and human contact was equally restricted and founded on ancient tradition. And even today this applies to some extent, especially to such matters as good manners and hospitality, for which the Celt has been renowned down the centuries, to the amazement even of the classical commentators on ancient Gaulish manners. Travellers have always been astonished at the unquestioning generosity of the Highlander to the stranger; the custom of always leaving a portion 'for the man on the hill', i.e. the chance guest, is widely observed. This was one of the many features of the Highland temperament that so amazed Dr Johnson on his tour. The stranger had only to arrive at even the poorest dwelling, to be given a portion of whatever happened to be available. For example, Boswell tells us:

> At Auchnasheal, we sat down on a green turf-seat at the end of a house; they brought us out two wooden dishes of milk, which we tasted. One of them was frothed like a syllabub.

Again, at an inn in Glenelg:

> This inn was furnished with not a single article that we could either eat or drink; but Mr Murchison, factor to the Laird of MacLeod in Glenelg, sent us a bottle of rum and some sugar, with a polite message, to acquaint us, that he was very sorry that he did not hear of us till we had passed his house, otherwise he should have insisted on our sleeping there that night; and that, if he were not obliged to set out for Inverness early next morning, he would have waited upon us. — Such extraordinary attention from this gentleman, to entire strangers, deserves the most honourable commemoration.

Martin records the welcome accorded by the natives of the remote island of Ronay told to him by a visiting minister from the Outer Isles. One of the natives demonstrated his high regard for the visitor by making a turn about him sunwise, blessing him and wishing him all happiness. Martin wished to avoid this, to him, pagan welcome, but the natives insisted upon it. On the way to the village they passed three enclosures. As Morison, the minister, entered each of these, the inhabitants all saluted him shouting 'Traveller you are welcome here'. A house had been chosen for his lodging. There was a bundle of straw on the floor for the minister to sit on. After a short, general discourse the natives went back to their homes and each man killed a sheep; five in all were killed. There were only five families on the entire island. The skins of the sheep were kept whole and flayed from the neck to the tail so that they formed a sort of sack. The skins were then filled with barley meal and this was given to the minister as a gift. Morison's servant was also presented with some bags of meal, as he was also a traveller. Such was the sacredness of the stranger and the traveller in the eyes of the Highlanders to whom hospitality was almost a religion.

Martin has some interesting information to give about the natives of this little island. He testifies to their devoutness; every Sunday morning they met in the chapel to repeat the Lord's Prayer, the Creed and Ten Commandments (having no resident minister to preach to them). Their houses were built of stone and thatched with straw; the thatch was secured by means of straw ropes, and these were weighted down with stones. The only language spoken was Gaelic, and the people dressed, apparently, like the natives of Lewis. All the people died off when some sailors landed on the island and stole the bull; without it their only source of produce was taken from them; a new colony was planted there later, but it is not recorded by Martin how this fared.

Another instance of the widespread tradition of hospitality in the Highlands is given by Martin when he says, of North Uist:

There was never an Inn here till of late, and now there is but one, which is not at all frequented, for eating, but only for drinking. The fine hospitality of the natives rendered an eating-house unnecessary.

Many, and elaborate daily customs are recorded by Martin and other writers, some of obvious extreme antiquity. He says, for example, that it was an ancient custom which was still in operation in his day, that when a group of men went into a house to do business, or to drink, the door of the house was left open and a rod was put across it; by this, it was understood that no person without rank may approach the house; if anyone should be ill-mannered enough to remove this rod and enter without invitation, he would cause serious affront to the company assembled within. Severe punishment was meted out to the offender by the gathering.

Martin also notes a custom which, in his day, was only observed by old people; this was the tradition of swearing by the chief or laird's hand. 'When a debate arises between two persons, if one of them assert the matter by your Father's Hand, they reckon it a great indignity; but if they go a degree higher, and out of spite say, by your Father and Grandfather's Hand, the next word is commonly accompanied by a blow.' In Martin's observations, as in those of writers on the Celts down the ages, orators always held an elevated place in society. Their houses and villages were regarded as sanctuaries and they had precedence even over medical doctors. Martin says that after the Druids had become extinct the orators were employed to preserve the genealogies of the noble families — always an important Highland activity. These were recited at important public occasions such as the succession of a chief, or his marriage or the birth of an heir. As in the distant past, anything requested by these orators was given to them, more out of fear of satire — a powerful and much-dreaded weapon — than out of respect. By Martin's time, however, these people had lost their effective power and only received a pittance.

Cures, tabus, and social customs are all closely intermingled in Highland life; there were days for doing things, and days for not doing things. For example, on the island of Gigha it was considered unlucky to bury people on a Friday. On the other hand, only a Friday would be suitable for the performance of certain cures. The healing of *màm* (*fàireagan na h-achlais*), swelling of the glands, must be undertaken on a Friday by certain gifted people, using specific methods. A magical incantation was apparently whispered over the blade of a knife or axe — steel was an essential ingredient in the cure — which was then held close to the mouth, and finally the blade was placed upon the swollen part. The swelling was then crossed and divided into nine or some other odd number; each time one of these divisions of the swelling was crossed with the steel, the blade was pointed towards a hill, the name of which began with *màm* and not the more usual *ben*. In this way the swelling of sickness was transferred to the natural swelling of the hill and this performance was believed to be an infallible cure. When the swelling was divided up and counted in this way, the blade was pointed towards the ground and the following words were said: 'The pain be in the ground and the affliction in the earth.' Martin records an interesting remedy for fever which was used in the island of Colonsay. A certain man, a member of whose family was ill with a fever, went to Martin to borrow his Bible so that he could fan the patient's face with it; at once, the sick person began to improve. This was apparently a recognised method of healing the sick.

Martin records a tradition connected with the preservation of boundaries which is of considerable interest. In Skye, people laid a quantity of burnt wood ash on the ground, and over these they placed large stones. A somewhat barbarous means of making each new generation aware of where the traditional boundaries were situated was as follows. Some boys from the villages on either side of the boundary were carried there and soundly whipped so that they should never forget the place; this, when the time came, they themselves did to their own offspring. Martin mentions that a boundary between the villages of Ose and Groban was being disputed at one time; when the stones were lifted and ashes were found there, the controversy was decided.

Charms were widely used, not only for the protection of the stock, the dwelling and its inmates, but against specific mishaps, including drowning and death in battle. The following translation of a Gaelic charm collected from an old man in Mull, about 1800, is given by Campbell in his book on Witchcraft and is important enough to quote here in full:

> For himself and for his goods,
> The charm Bridget put round Dorgill's daughter,
> The charm Mary put round her Son,
> Between her soles and her neck,
> Between her breast and her knee,

Between her eye and her hair;
The sword of Michael be on thy side,
The shield of Michael on thy shoulder;
There is none between sky and earth
Can overcome the King of grace.
Edge will not cleave thee,
Sea will not drown thee,
Christ's banners round thee,
Christ's shadow over thee;
From thy crown to thy sole,
The charm of virtue covers thee.
You will go in the King's name,
And come in your Commander's name;
Thou belongest to God and all His powers.
I will make the charm on Monday,
In a narrow, sharp, thorny space;
Go, with the charm about thee,
And let no fear be on thee!
Thou wilt ascend the tops of cliffs,
And not be thrown backwards;
Thou art the calm Swan's son in battle,
Thou wilt stand amid the slaughter;
Thou wilt run through five hundred,
And thy oppressor will be caught;
God's charm be about thee!
People go with thee!

A smith in Mull was alleged to have got this charm from his father. He subsequently enlisted in the army and fought in some 30 battles. He came home unscathed; although he had in fact been struck by bullets, the charm rendered them powerless. This is only

Euffignieux eye

one example of many beliefs in the power of the *sian,* 'charm' against war.

Charms were also used for the cloth when it had been waulked, or shrunk. It was then neatly folded and laid on the table, and the waulking women gathered round and sang a charm over the material. As they sang, they lifted their hands together and beat the cloth, turning it over after each repetition of the charm.

Callanish

— 6 —

Life and Death

DEATH HAS always been one of the main preoccupations of the Celt; this no doubt stems ultimately from the cult of graves, ancestor worship, and the belief that the burial mound was either one of the entrances to the Otherworld, or the place in which the departed continued his ghostly life, and must be propitiated with various rites and offerings. Even the practice of placing flowers on the graves of the departed must be an almost instinctive continuation of the widespread and archaic practice of honouring and placating the dead with offerings. Burial and everything associated with death has by no means always been a purely gloomy affair, and the social gathering and meal provided by the bereaved after the funeral is probably likewise a carry-over from the old funeral games and merry-making which were an integral part of Celtic burial traditions until comparatively recent times. Very often the merry-making got out of hand and bitter quarrels ending in blows were by no means uncommon phenomena. Funeral customs differed in the Highlands from area to area and according to the religion – Catholic or

107

Protestant — of the people concerned. Belief in the ghost of the departed person was very strong, and, on occasion, the spirit could be very dangerous to the living. In some districts it was believed that the soul stayed close to the corpse until after burial; the body must be watched day and night. This custom was known as the 'late wake', and very unChristian activities could take place during this period of watching over the dead, and keeping guard on the restless spirit. All sorts of tricks were practised, games of leaping and wrestling were indulged in, riddles asked and answered, music known as the *coronach* or 'lament' was played, and the whole sad situation was treated with an almost callous revelry.

Pennant describes how, on the death of a Highlander, the body was stretched on a board, and covered with a coarse linen wrapper; the relatives of the deceased then placed a wooden platter on the breast of the corpse, containing a small quantity of salt and earth, not mixed together, but kept separate. The earth was symbolic of the corruptible body; the salt was the emblem of the indestructible spirit. All fire was extinguished in the room in which the corpse lay; in Pennant's time it was regarded as such a bad omen for a cat or a dog to pass over the corpse, that the poor creature must immediately be killed. Pennant also refers to the Late-Wake; he records that on the evening after the death of any person, the relations and friends of the deceased were in the habit of meeting at the house, accompanied by the music of bagpipe or fiddle. The nearest of kin — wife, son or daughter — would open a melancholy ball, dancing and at the same time weeping. This would continue until dawn. The younger people present treated the occasion with much more levity. Should the corpse remain unburied in the house for two days, the same rites would be observed on the second night. 'Thus, Scythian-like, they rejoice at the deliverance of their friends out of this life of misery.' Pennant also observes that the *coranach*, or singing at funerals, was still in use in his day in some places. These songs were generally eulogies of the deceased, or a recital of the valiant deeds of him and his ancestors. Pennant comments:

> I had not the fortune to be present at any in North Britain, but formerly assisted at one in the south of Ireland, where it was performed in the fullness of horror. The cries are called by the Irish the *Ulogohne* and *Húllulu*, two words extremely expressive

of the sound uttered on these occasions and being of Celtic stock, Etymologists would swear to be the origin of the ὀλολυγών of the Greeks and *Ululatus* of the Latins. It was my fortune to arrive at a certain town in Kerry at the time that a person of some distinction departed this life; my curiosity led me to the house, where the funeral seemed conducted in the purest classical form . . . when the time approached for carrying the corpse out, the cry was re-doubled — a numerous band of females waiting in the outer court to attend the hearse and to pay (in chorus) the last tribute of their voices. The habit of this sorrowing train and the neglect of their persons, were admirably suited to the occasion: their robes were black and flowing, resembling the ancient *palla*; their feet naked, their hair long and dishevelled . . . the corpse was carried slowly along the verge of a most beautiful lake, the *ululatus* was continued, and the whole procession ended among the venerable ruins of an old abbey. But to return to North Britain. Midwives give new-born babes a small spoonful of earth and whisky as the first food they taste.

In certain places, Pennant records, 'the death of people is supposed to be foretold by the cries and shrieks of *Benshi* or the Fairies wife, uttered along the very path where the funeral is to pass; and what in Wales are called corps candles, are often imagined to appear and foretell mortality'.

Martin relates how the natives of the island of Eigg did not allow Protestants to come to their burials. He also mentions some small chapels on the island of Benbecula. One of these was called Nun's Town (*Baile nan Caillich*), for there were nunneries here 'in the time of popery'. Martin tells how the natives had recently discovered a stone vault on the east side of the town which was full of small bones. Some people would have it that they were the bones of birds, and others that they were the remains of pigmies. Sir Norman MacLeod was asked about them and he surmised that they were the bones of the illegitimate babies of the nuns. This greatly displeased the Catholics on the island; the vault was promptly closed up, and never again opened. Martin, who records a good deal about death customs and burials in the islands, tells us that the burial ground near the houses on the island of Borera was called the Monks Field, because all the monks that died in the islands to the north of Eigg were buried in this small piece of ground. Another island, Lingay, lying half a league south on the side of Borera is, according to Martin's observation, entirely moss covered with heather which afforded five peats in depth; even so, such was the sanctity of the island down the ages in the eyes of the natives of the islands that they dared not cut fuel in it, rich in peats though it was.

Shaw, in recording traditions from Moray in the eighteenth century, gives us some information about death customs in his day. Although, like so many collectors of folk belief, he was a minister of the Church, and therefore somewhat ashamed and censorious of the customs of his fellow-countrymen, he did write them down faithfully as he found them, at a time when they were fully active. The area with which he was particularly concerned extended from the mouth of the River Spey to the borders of Lochaber, and from the Moray Firth to the Grampian hills. It was commonly said in Moray at this time that at death one passed into the *saoghal thall*, 'the Yonder World'; today, in modern Gaelic communities it is never said of a person who has died, *bhàsaich e* (*bàs*, 'death'); this is reserved for animals. Of a human being people say *chaochail e*, 'he changed', or *shiubhail e*, 'he travelled', which is very similar to Shaw's eighteenth-century observation. He says, somewhat sternly of the Highlanders of his day: 'they retain many heathenish practices', which included music and dancing at lyke-wakes and burials; these sports were commonplace. The nearest relations of the deceased were apparently the first to dance. He also mentions the mourning women (*bean tuirim*) who were employed to chant the *coronach,* or lament, reciting the heroic deeds, the hunting prowess, the largesse and so on of the deceased, in true archaic Celtic fashion. Shaw also notes that it was commonplace in Moray in his day for people to make a sunwise (*deiseal*) procession round the church at marriages, funerals and the churching of women, that is, their first visit to church after the birth of a child — before this they were held to be unclean.

It was also at one time widely believed that on the night of the day that a child was baptised, the baby was neither bathed nor washed. This was to make sure that the evil-averting baptismal water was not washed off the child before it had slept under its protection. Very often the holy water used at the ceremony was bottled up and kept as a precious remedy for various disorders. Female children must not be baptised with the same water as that used for a male child, otherwise they would, according to popular superstition, grow beards. One minister recorded an experience he himself had when he was about to baptise a female baby with the water with which he had just baptised a male child. The grandmother apparently snatched away the baptismal bowl and filled it with fresh holy water, lest the girl should grow up and have a beard. In many districts it was considered to be unlucky if a child was not baptised within a year of its birth. Another ancient belief of the Highlanders was in the efficacy of a cold plunge and in earlier times in the Highlands as soon as the baby was born it was plunged into a running stream and then wrapped in a warm blanket. This is almost identical with the custom recorded by Strabo for Gaul where mothers of newly-born infants plunged them into the ice-cold waters of some river in order to make them strong and lusty.

Another widespread Highland custom was to make the baby swallow a large quantity of fresh butter after birth. At this time, the power of the fairies was much feared and before baptism it must be protected against this dangerous race of beings, and other supernatural creatures. One method was to take a basket half filled with bread and cheese, and wrapped in a clean linen cloth. The child was laid on top of this package as if it were in a cradle. The basket was then lifted up by the oldest female member of the family, carried three times round the fire, and then suspended for a few seconds above it. After that, the infant was put back in its cradle, and the bread and cheese shared out amongst those present as a guarantee of their health for the coming year. Another superstition recorded, like those above by MacGregor early in this century, was that, soon after the birth of a child, and after all the correct ritual had been observed, a dish containing a mixture of oat-meal and water was made, and each person present must take three horn-spoonfuls in order to bring protection on the infant. The custom was still vestigially extant in Perthshire when MacGregor wrote, and may, of course, have continued long after, unknown to the minister. There too, it was traditionally believed that, until she had been kirked, everything a new mother touched was unclean. Another protection given to the newly-born child, this time against worldly ills, was to twine a straw rope three times sunwise round the infant's body when it was being washed, in the name of the Trinity. This rope was then cut into three parts and as long as these pieces did not re-unite, the child would be safe from the curse of epilepsy; Carmichael recorded this custom in the islands.

Birth, marriage and death have always, in the Highlands, as elsewhere, been the vital foci of mankind, and it is natural that these three major experiences should attract much belief and superstitious practice. Sometimes, when experienced medical attention failed, folk remedies to facilitate a birth were used, apparently, on occasion, with dramatic results. Carmichael records one remarkable and well-authenticated instance of this, which occurred at Rosehall in Sutherland in 1908. The birth was attended by an experienced and reliable nurse; it was a very difficult one, and the nurse, who was alone, could do nothing further herself to assist the desperately ill mother, except wait for the arrival of the doctor. The girl was in a terrible state of pain and finally her mother resorted to a traditional remedy for a delayed birth. She filled a small basin with water, no doubt from some special holy well, and into this water she placed a number of rings and brooches of gold and silver; she then stirred them around in the water. The girl in labour was by this time on the point of death; her mother held the basin to her dying daughter's lips and made her drink three mouthfuls of the water, each mouthful in the name of the Father, Son and Holy Ghost — the three persons of the Trinity. Almost immediately afterwards the child was born. The doctor arrived shortly after, and the girl recovered. Although the baby was born before the doctor could reach the house, the birth was extremely easy. The nurse was completely baffled by this experience and had no idea what had made this strange process successful and had, in spite of herself, to believe that some strange occult power had been at work.

MacGregor notes a remarkable marriage custom which was practised in Easter Ross. Once the wedding festivities were over the couple must go to be kirked on the first Sunday after the marriage. If several weddings had taken place in the same week, things became very complicated. In this instance, when the sermon was over, the newly-wed couples, without waiting for the benediction, would rush from the church and make for home; the couple to reach home first would then be certain of a happy and prosperous life; those left behind were more likely to be the victims of misfortune.

Even until comparatively recently, a Highland wedding was an elaborate and lengthy affair. It could last for several days and much ritual attended it. There was a wedding feast consisting of cold mutton and fowl and all the usual dairy produce, scones, cheese, oatcakes and so on, contributed by all the neighbours; whisky was drunk and the couple were toasted by all. After the feast, a riotous dance ensued, and the bridal couple had to take the lead in the *Wedding Reel*. The festivities continued for most of the night and often for several days, and there was much sport and fun and ribald humour.

To return to the most serious of these three stages of man's life, MacGregor records that in Ross-shire it was believed that the soul did not finally leave the body until the corpse had been laid in the grave — this was, in fact, a very widespread Highland belief. In Perthshire it was held that, at the moment of death, whether it be natural or the result of an accident, the soul could be actually seen leaving the body in the shape of a small insect such as a bee or a butterfly. This belief in the soul in animal form is very widespread and ancient, and like so much else goes back to the earliest Celtic traditions.

Martin records that in Bernera, Harris, there was a freshwater lake called Loch Bruist, in which there were small islets, rich in fowl of many species. In the island of Taransay, there were two chapels, one dedicated to Saint Tarran and the other to Saint Keith. He mentions an ancient tradition amongst the natives that a man must not be buried in Saint Tarran's nor a woman in Saint Keith's — if this were to be done, the corpse would be found above the ground on the day following its interment.

Amongst the many fascinating death and burial traditions Martin notes is that of a grave found on the little island of Ensay which lies between Bernera and the main land of Harris. He mentions an old chapel, and he says there was 'lately discovered a grave in the west end of the island in which was found a pair of scales made of brass, and a little hammer, both of which were finely polished'. The burial of grave goods in Christian contexts is rare, and this unusual interment may thus have been of great antiquity.

The Highlanders had, and have, a deep, widespread belief in death warnings of all kinds — portents which indicated the imminent decease of some member of a family or community. These, quite naturally, always give rise to superstitious dread, and there is deep unease until the omen has been fulfilled. Certain clans and their septs, as well as individual families, had death warnings known to, and peculiar to, themselves. Immediately before the death, someone was certain to see or hear the eerie warning. Campbell, in his book on Witchcraft, gives several examples of these, and the superstition still continues in certain remote areas where the old beliefs die hard. Before a member of the Breadalbane family died, for instance, a bull would be heard at night roaring on the hillside. As the animal ascended the hillside, the noise grew fainter and finally died away altogether as the portenteous animal passed over the top. A folk

Pictish bulls

legend accounts for this manifestation: apparently the head of a bull was at one time brought in to a feast as a signal for the massacre of a number of MacGregors whom Breadalbane had asked to his castle as guests. A small bird – a common death portent – was the sign of the death of a member of the MacLachlan clan. Some families were warned of approaching bereavement by a strange whistling sound; others by a light which glowed like a candle. There were countless other variations on the basic theme – screaming, wailing, the sound of someone sobbing, and so on. These death warnings were quite distinct from ordinary earthly sounds or objects, and when they occurred the air became deathly cold – another common feature in connection with supernatural happenings. Sometimes before a nobleman was to die a light like a meteor could be seen in the sky (*dreug*); this would move from the house where the death was to occur and make its way to the place of burial. This was invariably the route to be taken by the funeral procession.

As mentioned above, a feature of death and burial which survived until modern times was the employment of professional female mourners; such a woman was known in Gaelic as the *bean tuirim,* 'the weeping woman'. Carmichael gives us some valuable information both about death customs in general and about this professional class of mourners. Apparently, in the island of Lismore, the place over which a funeral procession travels is regarded both as sacred, and as a right of way. In Barra a corpse was left unburied for 48 hours alone; in Uist it was retained in the house from three to five nights. The *seis* or *seisig-bhàis*, 'death-wailing', could be heard in the house in which the death had taken place. The *tuiream*, 'lament', was the mourning in the open air after the doleful funeral procession. Some pipers were renowned for their laments at funerals. Carmichael records that the word *gul* or *gal* was a term which was applied to this archaic custom of professional mourning. By 1904 it had become redundant in Scotland although it was still in vogue in Ireland, where it was called *caoineadh*, the well-known anglicized word 'keening'. Carmichael was able to persuade an old Barra woman to demonstrate this almost lost art, and his description of the whole performance is most impressive. The occasion was that of the tragic burial of a young fisherman:

The scene was remarkable; below and right before us on its tidal rock stood the magnificent ruin of Ciosmal Castle, the ancient residence of MacNeil of Barra, and beyond this for twelve miles out to sea lay one behind another the isles of the Atlantic, usually wild and foamy, like lions at bay, this day peaceful and calm as lambs tired of play. The *bean tuirim* was tall and handsome, though somewhat gaunt and bony, with long features and long arms. At first she was reluctant to sing, but by degrees she came to use her voice to the full and the result was striking in the extreme. She and I carried the body as it was carried in simple fashion on three staves by a man at either end of each. The woman rehearsed the grief, the bitter grief, of the winsome young widow, the bitter cries of young helpless children, asking who would now bring them the corn from the *breird,* the meal from the mill, the fish from the sea and the birds from the rocks? Who indeed? No one now, since he was laid low. She then rehearsed the sorrows of the poor and the needy, the friendless and the aged whom he had been wont to help.

Carmichael's record of this procedure is an important description of this deeply-rooted and ancient tradition, which, in his day, had so very nearly been lost to posterity. In Tiree, the *bean tuirim* was still employed until the mid-nineteenth century. There was seemingly ill-feeling between the last keening woman there and one of her neighbours, Domhnall Ruadh, 'Red Donald'. When she last met him alive she told him she would make him live for ever. He died soon after that and she took her place at the head of the procession, according to custom. She had, however, hidden a cat under her cloak, and at the end of each eulogistic and elegaic passage, the cat mewed loudly. All the young people present thought this was very amusing, but the older people were shocked at the crudeness of her malice towards the deceased. As a result, she was never asked to keen again, and the custom died out. In 1872 Carmichael collected the following tradition from Catherine Pearson of Barra; each township had its own midwife and mourning-woman. These essential members of the community were provided by the township with free grazing and fodder. They were protected in every possible way so that they were able to perform their vital duties whenever called upon. Carmichael then gives a variety of incidents and laments which are invaluable to those who are interested in the rich lore of Gaelic Scotland, now so rapidly disappearing.

Cockerel

═◦ 7 ◦═

The Seasons:

Calendar Festivals and the Daily Round

IN THE WILD, isolated hills, glens and islands of the Scottish Highlands, where man is utterly dependent on the seasons and the forces of nature, there flourished from earliest times a rich folklore connected with lucky and unlucky days and months, and rites and incantations to twist the arm of the ever-waiting hostile forces into benevolence rather than malevolence; to ensure good harvests from the land and the sea, healthy stock, and an abundance of all the produce upon which the simple lives of the Highlanders depended. The ancient seasonal festivals survive vestigially in some areas, while even a century ago they were still a vital part of the life of the community, an insurance against ill-luck and the ever-lurking powers of darkness. Although these calendar feasts were regarded as great social affairs, relieving, for a brief spell the hardship and monotony of more or less subsistence living, they also had a fundamental religious connotation; at first pagan, and then Christian, subtly interwoven with archaic non-Christian rites. Labour too, of an everyday nature, required blessing and protection, and it is in this

117

whole field of activity that some of the most unique and fascinating folklore and customs of the British Isles is to be found.

The very names for the quarters of the Celtic year are pre-Christian. *Earrach*, 'Spring'; *Samhradh*, 'Summer'; *Foghara*, 'Harvest'; *Geamhradh*, 'Winter'. And, in the main, the ancient pagan quarterly festivals, for purification and good fortune, have continued to be practised at the same calendar seasons, with the inclusion of *Nollaig*, 'Christmas' as a Christian feast, although the *Bliadhna Ùr*, 'New Year', has always taken precedence over *Nollaig* as far as festivities are concerned. As in the ancient Celtic world, in the Highlands night is reckoned as preceding the day, and periods of time are counted in terms of nights rather than days. The main calendar festivals are, then, as follows.

Nollaig, 'Christmas'

Although Christmas was not the most important festival in the Gaelic communities of the western Highlands, it was observed; today it is much more the commercialised festival that it has become all over Britain, but in Carmichael's day, the old traditions were still observed, although even at that time they were rapidly dying out. Up to the last century, Christmas chants were very numerous. Carmichael comments that, where they were still recited, it was the boys of the township who performed the ceremonies attendant on the chants. He records that on Christmas Eve groups of boys used to go from house to house, and from township to township chanting the old traditional songs. They were known in Gaelic as *gillean Nollaig*, 'Christmas lads', or, alternatively *goisearan*, 'guisers'. They dressed up in white, wearing long, surplice-like shirts and tall white hats. When they entered a dwelling-house they would immediately lift up any child they found there. If there was no child in any particular house, a substitute of some kind was used; the baby, or imitation child being known as *Crist* or *Cristean*, 'the Little Christ'. The infant was placed on the skin of a male lamb, a creature without blemish, which was first specially consecrated for this purpose. It was then carried three times round the fire in a *deiseal* ('sunwise') direction, the leader of the boys carrying it, while all the boys followed, singing a chant known as the *Christmas Hail*. The sacred lamb-skin was called *uilim*. Afterwards, offerings were made to the babe. Then the people of the house gave the Christmas lads food and drink and a feast followed. Martin notes that the inhabitants of Harris, who were all Protestants, observed the festival of Christmas, but provides no further details. He also makes the same comment about the Protestant island of North Uist, likewise with no attendant details. He makes an interesting comment on the festival customs of the island of Oronsay; he notes that, although the men kept the festivals of Christmas, Easter and Good Friday, the women only observed the festivity of the nativity of the Virgin Mary.

Carmichael records a very interesting tradition of Christmas for the stock, This was known as *Nollaig do Spréidh,* and continued, in some areas at least, until the mid-nineteenth century. For example, apparently on the island of Lismore, it was the custom to provide each animal with a special breakfast on Christmas morning. Horses and cattle were given a sheaf of corn from the stall; sheaves of corn were spread out for the sheep in the fields; the pigs and the poultry likewise had a special feast. If there was a suitable tree near to the dwelling-house a sheaf of oats was hung up on it. If not, a wooden pole was erected and the sheaf was fastened to the top of the pole — a custom reminiscent of the most archaic pagan practice. Carmichael also records that in Breadalbane the cows were believed to go down on their knees in their byres at midnight on Christmas Eve. Another very odd Highland belief was that all the bees would leave their hives at three o'clock on Christmas morning, to return again immediately.

Oidhche Challuinn, 'New Year's Eve'

The eve of New Year's Day was one of supreme importance in the Highlands and Islands of the West and took precedence even over Christmas. It was a time of much ceremony and gaiety, but underneath the levity lies a sinister hint of the old ritual and sacrificial nature of the festival. The Eve of New Year was known as *Oidhche Challuinn,* and New Year's Day as *Là Challiunn.* First-footing is still carried out, as in other parts of the Highlands, although, as elsewhere, it is a dying custom. Up to the beginning of the century at least, the festivities of New Year's Eve were fully in operation and people went round the houses in every township carrying dried cow-hides and chanting special rhymes continuously. They beat the skins with sticks and struck the walls of the houses

with clubs; this ritual was believed to have an apotropaic effect and
to keep at bay fairies and evil spirits and hostile forces of every kind.
The part of the hide used was the loose flap of the beast's neck; this
was called in Gaelic *caisean-uchd*. This they used to singe in the fire
and present it to the members of the family, each in turn; every
member of the household was required to smell it as a charm against
all things evil and harmful. One example of the type of rhyme
chanted is as follows:

> Great good luck to the house,
> Good luck to the family,
> Good luck to every rafter of it,
> And to every worldly thing in it.
>
> Good luck to horses and cattle,
> Good luck to the sheep,
> Good luck to everything,
> And good luck to all your means.
>
> Luck to the good-wife,
> Good luck to the children,
> Good luck to every friend,
> Great fortune and health to all.

Carmichael gives the following example of a Hogmanay rhyme:

> Tonight is the hard night of Hogmanay,
> I am come with a lamb to sell —
> The old fellow yonder sternly said
> He would strike my ear against a rock.
>
> The woman, better of speech, said
> That I should be let in;
> For my food and for my drink,
> A morsel due and something with it.

Apparently lads with no better rhyme used to chant the
following:

> I have no dislike of cheese,
> I have no disgust of butter,

> But a little sip of barley bree
> I am right willing to put down!

The young people used to travel in groups round their own townships. In different areas, different rites would be performed at each house, but some form of *Duan Challuinn*, 'Hogmanay Poem', would always be chanted. There were two types of visitation; in one instance the *duan* was recited outside the house and the chant described the ritual of approaching and entering the house. Another *duan* was sung after the house had been entered, when the *caisean Calluig*, 'Hogmanay Hide', was beaten. This is also called the *Caisean a'Bhuilg*, 'Hide of the Bag'. The basic form of the ritual was universal in spite of regional variants in ritual and terminology. These old practices have virtually died out, but the ancient and pagan ritual discernible in them requires no comment. The boys who took part in these rites were known as *gillean Callaig*, 'Hogmanay lads', and the ceremony was performed at night. One of the boys was covered with the hide of a bull to which the horns and hooves were still attached. When they came to a house in some areas they climbed to the flat edge of the thatched roof and ran round it in a sunwise direction, the boy, or man, wearing the hide would shake the horns and hooves, and the others would strike at the bull-man with sticks. He was meant to be a frightening figure, and apparently the noise of this ritual beating and shaking of the hide was terrific. After this part of the ceremony was performed, the boys came down from the roof and recited their blatantly pagan chants; afterwards they were given hospitality in the house. The rhyme when the hide was in the process of being struck was as follows:

> Hogmanay of the sack,
> Hogmanay of the sack,
> Strike the hide,
> Strike the hide.
> Hogmanay of the sack,
> Hogmanay of the sack,
> Beat the skin,
> Beat the skin.
> Hogmanay of the sack,
> Hogmanay of the sack,

> Down with it! Up with it;
> Strike the hide.
> Hogmanay of the sack,
> Hogmanay of the sack,
> Down with it! Up with it!
> Beat the skin.
> Hogmanay of the sack,
> Hogmanay of the sack.

This ritual rhyme was, of course, chanted in Gaelic. Its very monotony imparted a certain eerie relentlessness to the ceremony. When it was finished, another carol or chant would be sung at the door of the house; this would praise – in anticipation – the generosity of the occupiers and would request entry and reward. In some areas the skin was singed by the man of the house, and the fumes it gave off were believed to have powers of purification, imparting health to all the family for the next twelve months. A New Year's Blessing, widely used and having a number of variants, could also be heard in both the islands and the Gaelic mainland. Pennant records, for the Dingwall region of Easter Ross, that he was told in the locality that on New Year's Day the people burned juniper before their cattle in order to protect them – another custom going back to Druidic times. He also learnt that on the first Monday of every quarter, the beasts were sprinkled with urine – a potent evil-averting substance.

Campbell, in his *Witchcraft,* gives other details of the Hogmanay ceremony. He says the hide of a cow was wrapped round the head of one of the men and he went off, followed by the rest of the party who struck the hide with switches so that it made a booming sound, similar to the noise of a drum. Again, the procession went three times *deiseal,* or sunwise, round every house in each township, beating on the walls of the house and chanting their rhymes at the door. The amount of drink taken must have been very considerable and as the evening wore on, the noise and rowdiness must have been quite alarming. On entering each house every member of the party was offered refreshments of the traditional kind – oatmeal, bread and cheese, and meat, followed by a dram of whisky. The man of the house was then given the *caisean-uchd,* which Campbell describes as the breast-skin of a sheep which was wrapped round the point of a shinty stick; this was, as in the other instances, singed in the fire, and carried three times sunwise round the family, grasped in the right hand, and held to the nose of each person. This was the focal point of the ritual. Campbell also records that as many people who wished to do so could carry a *caisean,* and that it could be made of goat or deer skin as well as from the breast-skin of a sheep. The houses were decorated with holly in order to keep out the fairies, always a troublesome race; it was believed that if a boy were whipped with a branch of this plant it was an assurance that he would live for as many years as the drops of blood drawn by the sharp holly — a painful way of ensuring longevity! Cheese, which as we have seen, was believed to have magical properties was an important item of the festive fare and the cheese eaten on this occasion was referred to as the *Càise Calluinn,* the Christmas Cheese. A slice of it was preserved, and if this happened to have a hole through it, it was believed to have special virtues. This sacred slice was known as *laomacha,* and a person who had lost his way at any time during the ensuing twelve months had only to look through the hole in the slice and he would know where he was — this was especially valuable to one lost on the hill in mist. It was regarded as a very magical festival in every respect, and games of all kinds were played. Some of these were concerned with the endlessly-fascinating desire to find out who one's future husband or wife was destined to be. Sometimes the boys in the Hogmanay procession were preceded by a piper. No matter how long or short the chant was, some words at least must be recited. It was the tradition to keep the fire, which was usually 'smoored' or extinguished at night, alive all through New Year's Night. Only a friend might approach the sacred blaze, and the candles were likewise kept burning in the house.

This custom gave rise to another name for the festival, *Oidhche Choinnle,* 'Candlemas'. These various rites were performed in the belief that, by observing them, evil would be kept from the dwelling for the ensuing year. When the fire was being fuelled on this night, a special incantation was recited, but Campbell was unable to obtain an example of this. If the fire went out that night, it boded ill for the coming year, and no neighbour would provide kindling to light it on the following day. Ritual even accompanied the extinguishing or 'smooring' of the everyday fires; the putting out of the flames was called in Gaelic *smàladh an teine*. The main fuel used in the Highlands and Islands was, of course, peat; wood was scarce, and although much more coal is used today, peat is still burnt. The fire was not entirely extinguished but kept barely smouldering during the night. Until very recently the fire was in the centre of the floor of the so-called 'black' houses, and the embers were smoothed out evenly on the hearth; these were then covered over with large peats and ashes to prevent the fire from blazing up in the night, but to ensure easy kindling in the morning. The whole process was regarded with superstition, and was accompanied by many incantations. One incantation, taken down by Carmichael invokes:

> The Sacred Three
> To save,
> To shield,
> To surround
> The hearth,
> The house,
> The household,
> This eve,
> This night,
> Oh! this eve,
> This night,
> And every night,
> Each single night.

There are many variants of invocations for this important function of smooring the fire, all of a sacred nature, and going right back to the ancient pagan belief in the miraculous power of fire. The kindling in the morning, on which all domestic comfort depended, had its own repertoire of charms and incantations for blessing:

> I will raise the hearth-fire
> As Mary would.
> The encirclement of Bride and of Mary
> On the fire, and on the floor,
> And on the household all.
>
> Who are they on the bare floor?
> John and Peter and Paul.

Who are they by my bed?
The lovely Bride and her Fosterling.
Who are those watching over my sleep?
The fair loving Mary and her Lamb.
Who is that at the back of my head?
The Son of Life without beginning, without time.

Deeply and sincerely Christian as these devout Highlanders were, they managed to keep the essence of the old religion in being by turning from the many pagan gods and goddesses — although, as we have seen, some of these were retained underneath a veneer of Christianity — to the many saints and angels, as well as the Virgin and the Trinity, thus continuing to surround themselves with divine protection, of a Christian kind, but according to the ancient pre-Christian formulae.

To return to the important festival of New Year. Campbell, in his *Witchcraft*, notes that *Latha na Bliadhn' Ùr*, 'New Year's Day' was also known as the Day of Little Christmas. After the family had got up in the morning, the head of the house gave a dram of whisky to each member of the household; then a strange custom followed in some areas; a breakfast was provided of half-boiled sowens — austere fare for a festive occasion. This was supposed to bring luck to the household. Campbell does say that this tradition was not observed in Mull, Morvern or the Western Isles. Then each member of the family exchanged traditional greetings and did likewise with every person they met. The boys then went off to play shinty and meanwhile a late and luxurious breakfast was prepared. Apparently, no substance of any kind was allowed to be removed from the house on New Year's Day — dirty water, sweepings from the floor, ashes and so on. If a neighbour's fire had gone out one must not give fire from one's own house to them; this was regarded as one of the most unlucky things that could be done. It would ensure a death within that family during the coming year; it also gave power to the black witches to take away the produce from the cattle. No woman should enter the house first on this portentous day.

Là Fèill Bhrìde, St Bride's Day

This most important festival is of particular interest in that not only has an ancient Celtic calendar festival been taken over into

Christianity, but a pagan goddess, Bride, or Brigit, has become a Christian saint, and in the Hebrides is held to be the midwife of the Virgin Mary. St Bride's feast-day is on 1 February, the time of one of the four great calendar festivals of the pagan Celtic year — *Imbolc*, a pastoral feast to celebrate lactation of the ewes, which began at that time. The saint was deeply loved in the Highlands, and until the last century very elaborate ritual was associated with her special day. In origin, the daughter of the Irish god, the *Dagda* (*Deagh Dia*, 'Good god'), and envisaged, like so many Celtic deities in triple form, she was also venerated in Celtic Europe, and gave her name in the form *Brigantia*, 'the High One', to the powerful confederacy of Celtic tribes in North Britain, the Brigantes, 'Devotees of Brigantia'. It is clear that she was a very important Celtic deity and a kind of Celtic Minerva. She was taken over into Christianity as St Brigit of Kildare, and her association with the land and the stock are always stressed in the Early Lives. A perpetual fire was kept burning in her honour at Kildare, constantly attended by nine Virgins. As the midwife of the supreme birth, she was much invoked in the Highlands by women in child-bed who sought her assistance in an easy and safe delivery. Very complex and elaborate ceremony took place on 1 February. Carmichael records that at one time, in the Catholic islands, the genealogy or *sloinntearachd* — always a passion amongst the Celts — of Bride was recited; it was chanted, and believed to be helpful in a variety of situations. Hymns were also sung to the goddess-saint on her feast day, but even in Carmichael's time, there were only fragmentary folk memories of them extant. The day was known in Gaelic as *Là Féill Bhrìde*, 'St Brigit's Feast Day'.

Bath matres

A legend was current in the Hebrides as to how the saint delivered Christ in the stable in Bethlehem; immediately after his birth she placed three drops of spring water on his brow, in the name of the Trinity. For this reason, people used to say, she is called *Muime Chriosda*, 'the Foster-mother of Christ'. He in his turn was known as *Dalta Bride* 'the Foster-Son of Bride'. This is an extremely important relationship in the Highlands, the tradition of fosterage being deeply rooted in Celtic traditions from earliest times, and the bond between foster-mother and foster-son being almost closer than that of parent and child. Carmichael, who made an invaluable contribution to our knowledge of Highland folklore and custom when he collected these vestigial remains of a once-elaborate ritual, records that when a woman was in labour, the midwife would go to her door, place her hands on the jambs, and beg Bride to enter by saying:

> Bride! Bride! come in,
> Thy welcome is truly made,
> Give thou relief to the woman.
> And give the conception to the Trinity.

An easy birth was believed to indicate that the saint was well-disposed towards the family; a difficult delivery suggested the opposite. The midwife placed three drops of pure water on the new-born infant's brow, just as Bride is alleged to have done to the baby Christ. On Saint Bride's Day eve, all the girls of each township used to make a sheaf of corn into a corn dolly; this they would then dress and decorate with shells and whatever flowers and greenery might be in bloom at the time. One particularly beautiful shell was kept and placed over the heart of the doll. This was intended to represent the Star of Wonder shining over Bethlehem. The doll was called *Bride* or *Brideag*, 'Little Bride, or Brigit'; it was then carried in procession to the accompaniment of a song in honour of the patron saint of childbirth. All the girls had to wear white dresses and their hair unbound. During the procession they would carry the doll to each household, and every person had to give a present to Bride and make obeisance to her; the gift need have no real value — it could be a shell, a flower, a pretty pebble, but *some* offering must be made. The mother of each household baked a special cake or bannock, or a cheese or roll of butter, which she presented to the image. Having gone round all the houses in the township, the girls would take all they had collected to one particular house, and make the *Féis Brìde*, 'Bride's Feast'. Once inside, the door was firmly secured, the windows were barred and the image of the saint was placed in the centre of the room. Carmichael records that, after a while, the boys of the township would come to the house and, with humility, ask for permission to honour Bride. After some ritual altercation, they were finally allowed to come in and to pay honour to the figure. After that general merry-making broke out, including dancing and feasting, games, tricks and pranks of every kind and the fun went on all through the night. At dawn all present in the house would form a circle and sing a special hymn in honour of Bride, the foster-mother of Christ. Then what was left of the feast was distributed among the poor women of the locality.

This custom was not confined to the Highlands, but is also known from Ireland, and was probably widely practised in the Celtic world, the Christian having supplanted the pagan rites. Away from the coasts, the dollies were decorated with very complex designs made of straw. Apparently, in Ireland, pins, bits of stone, needles, straws and other small items were presented to the image. This is particularly interesting because pins of every kind were the common offerings made to the mother goddess for fertility and ease in childbirth throughout the pagan Celtic world, as elsewhere. The cake baked on the first day of spring was called *Bonnach Brìde;* other cakes which formed part of the ritual of the annual festivals likewise had their appropriate names. Carmichael records that the older women had their own role to play at the Bride celebrations. On this joyous day, the first day of spring, they would fashion an oblong basket of straw in the shape of a cradle, which was known as Bride's Bed. This they decorated with care. A sheaf of oats was customarily formed into the shape of a woman, and again, decorated with shells, semi-precious stones and ribbons. This figure was called *Dealbh Brìde*, 'Bride's Image'. After that the women invite the goddess to enter her bed and they place the figure in it. She was traditionally given a wand made of peeled wood from some evil-averting tree. Next the ashes were 'smoored' on the hearth. On the morning of the next day, the whole family would examine the ashes first thing; if the marks of Bride's wand could be discerned, the omens were good. If these were lacking, then Bride's displeasure was allegedly manifested and sorrow to the family in the coming year was to be expected. In order to propitiate the goddess-saint, a cockerel was buried alive at a point where three streams meet and incense was burnt on the hearth that night. Another name for Bride's Day was *Là Cath Choileach* 'The Day of Cock-fighting'. Of particular interest from the viewpoint of Celtic mythology is the fact that on this sacred day the serpent was supposed to come forth from its hollow in the hills; a propitiatory hymn was sung to it. One version is as follows:

> Early on Bride's morn
> The serpent shall come from the hole,
> I will not molest the serpent,
> Nor will the serpent molest me.

There are several other versions of this strange hymn:

> The feast day of Bride,
> The daughter of Ivor shall come from the knoll,
> I will not molest the serpent,
> Nor will the serpent molest me.

Or

> On the Feast Day of Bride,
> The head will come off the caiteanach (?)
> The daughter of Ivor will come from the knoll
> With tuneful whistling.
>
> The serpent will come from the hole
> On the brown day of Bride,
> Though there should be three feet of snow
> On the flat surface of the ground.

The serpent is the daughter of Ivor – probably one of the legendary invaders of Ireland in the centuries before Christ. Although Solinus records in the second century that there were no serpents in Ireland, early Irish mythology is full of references to snakes and serpentiform monsters. Highland folklore knows many serpent legends, and, as Carmichael rightly points out, this hymn in connection with the saint-goddess Bride indicates vestigial serpent-worship. A very strange custom which seems to contradict the veneration of the snake took place on Bride's Day, where again the pagan elements in the Christian festival are very apparent; this was the pounding of the serpent in effigy. Carmichael actually witnessed the performance of this ritual in Skye and gave the following account of the archaic ceremony. The woman of the house who was then 84 years of age, on the morning of Bride's Day went to the fire and took a piece of peat from it. She took off one of her stockings, and, placing the peat in it, laid it on the threshold of the house and pounded it with the tongs. As she struck the peat she chanted, in Gaelic:

> This is the Day of Bride,
> The queen will come from the mound,
> I will not touch the queen,
> Nor will the queen touch me.

Like her Irish counterpart, Bride presided over the various seasons of the year; she was believed to bring life back to the earth after the dead months of winter, by means of her magic white wand. In Uist the flocks were dedicated to Bride on her sacred Day:

> On the Feast Day of beautiful Bride,
> The flocks are counted on the moor,
> The raven goes to prepare the nest,
> And again goes the rook.

It was traditional in Barra to cast lots for the fishing-grounds on Bride's Day, an event of great importance. There, the fishing-banks are well known and are divided according to the number of people engaged in long-line fishing. First of all the entire community would go to Church. During the Service, Bride's virtues were recited and she was accorded deep veneration. After the ceremonies in the Church, the men would go to the Church door and there cast lots for the fishing-banks. Bride to a great extent, held a position of affection amongst the people which was in some ways more powerful than that occupied by the Virgin Mary; and the antiquity of her cult throughout the Celtic world makes this fully understandable. A fascinating genealogy of the saint used to be chanted, full of early Irish names and superstitions which make quite clear that the old pagan associations of the saint were not forgotten, if not fully understood:

> The genealogy of the holy maiden Bride,
> Radiant flame of gold, noble foster-mother of Christ.
> Bride daughter of Dugall the brown,
> Son of Aodh, son of Art, son of Conn,
> Son of Crearer, son of Cis, son of Carmac, son of Carruin.
>
> Every day and every night
> That I say the genealogy of Bride,
> I shall not be killed, I shall not be harried,
> I shall not be put in cell, I shall not be wounded,
> Neither shall Christ leave me in forgetfulness.
>
> No fire, no sun, no moon shall burn me,
> No lake, no water, nor sea shall drown me,
> No arrow of fairy, nor dart of fay shall wound me,
> And I under the protection of my Holy Mary,
> And my gentle foster-mother is my beloved Bride.

The first three lines of the last verse show an astonishing archaism; they refer to the tradition of the threefold death, a motif known in early Irish literature. The victim is stabbed in a house, which is then set on fire; he rushes out to throw his burning body into water, whereupon he is drowned. This would seem to be a survival of the ancient Celtic custom of human sacrifice and to apply particularly to a passage from Lucan where he records that men were sacrificed to the great god Esus, 'Lord, Master', by being first of all stabbed, and then hung up in a tree; Taranis, 'The Thunderer', was propitiated by offering people to the fire; Teutates, 'God of the People', had his victims drowned in his honour. The motif of the threefold death thus had a long ancestry, and there would seem to be a lingering hint of it here when Bride is invoked as a protective force against burning, drowning and stabbing.

Diardaoin Chaluim-Chille, 'St Columba's Day'

In discussing Highland Calendar Festivals, we have seen how Pennant mentions that on the first Monday of every quarter the people in the Conon region used to sprinkle their cattle with urine — urine being widely believed to have strong apotropaic powers. He then goes on to mention that 'in some parts of the country is a rural sacrifice, different from that before-mentioned'. He observed that a cross was cut on some sticks, which were then dipped in pottage; the Thursday before Easter one of each of these were placed over the sheep-cot, the stable, or the cow-house, to protect the stock. Maundy Thursday was, of course, St Columba's Day — *Diardaoin Chaluim-Chille*, one of the best-loved of the Highland saints. The Day was observed in a variety of different ways throughout the Highlands. It was looked upon as a lucky day for all activities, including setting out on a journey. On the eve of St Columba's Day, the woman of the house used to make a bannock of oats or rye and she would place a small silver coin in this. The cake was then toasted in front of a fire which had been kindled from one of the sacred woods — oak, yew, or rowan. On Maundy Thursday the head of the house would take the cake and cut it into as many pieces as there were children in the family, all of the same size. These were placed in a basket and each child helped himself to a piece; the child who got the coin was given the crop of lambs for the year, or at least part of them. In coastal regions a very pagan practice occurred; offerings were made to some now obscure sea-god. This strange custom persisted down into the present century. In Lewis, for example, the god was called Shony, a corruption no doubt for some ancient pagan divine name. A man would wade up to his waist in the sea and pour ale into it at midnight on the Eve of Maundy Thursday; various chants are known, and one recorded by Carmichael is as follows:

> O God of the sea,
> Put weed in the drawing wave
> To enrich the ground,
> To shower on us food.

Everyone behind the man performing this ritual took up the chant; often the ceremony would be followed by food and drink and merry-making. The patently pagan custom was seriously frowned on by the Protestant Church, but persisted nevertheless. Thursday, because of its associations with St Columba, was always regarded as a lucky day, except, apparently, when Beltain fell on a Thursday. The following incantation used to be said on St Columba's Day:

> Thursday of Columba benign,
> Day to send sheep on prosperity,
> Day to send cow on calf,
> Day to put the web in the warp.
>
> Day to put coracle on the brine,
> Day to place the staff to the flag,
> Day to bear, day to die,
> Day to hunt the heights.
>
> Day to put horses in harness,
> Day to send herds to pasture,
> Day to make prayer efficacious,
> Day of my beloved, the Thursday,
> Day of my beloved, the Thursday.

Pennant notes that the Highlanders paid great attention to lucky and unlucky days in his time. He says that they regarded 14 May as an unlucky day; it fell on a Thursday during the period of his travels, and he says 'Thus Thursday is a black day for the present year'.

Di-Dòmhnuich-càisg, 'Easter'

Easter Sunday was observed in the Highlands by preparing and eating certain kinds of pan-cakes made of eggs, milk, meal or flour. The tradition of taking quantities of hard-boiled eggs dyed in various substances was also prevalent amongst the young; these were rolled and then eaten; this custom persists in many places to the present day. Good Friday was also observed, and in many areas the sanctity of this day was remembered throughout the year. For example, the time of the marking of the lambs was one thought to be fraught with potential evil and danger. Invocations and special rites were widely regarded as being necessary to avoid disaster. The marking was traditionally done on a Thursday, Saint Columba's Day. It was customary never to mark the lambs on a Friday, or to draw blood on that day. Carmichael records that the Highlanders tended never to use iron in any form on Friday. A blacksmith in Benbecula, and a Protestant not a Catholic, would, according to Carmichael, never open his smithy on a Friday. He used to say, apparently, that 'that was the least he could do to honour his Master'. The pieces cut from the lambs' ears were carefully buried beyond reach of bird or beast. It was believed that a certain plant grew from them, which was known as *gearradh-chluasach*; when this plant is ripe, it is cut, tied up in a bunch and hung from the couple above the door of the lamb cot. This custom still persisted until Carmichael's time.

Là Beltain, 'May Day'

Beltain was one of the most ancient calendar festivals of the Celtic year. It was sacred to the god Belinus, whose cult orbit stretched from the Italic Peninsula, across Europe and into the British Isles. The great Catuvellaunian leader in southern Britain, whose reign lasted some 40 years and ended shortly before the Claudian invasion in AD 43, bore the name of Cunobelinus — Hound of Belinus. And there is evidence that the mythological king in the story of *Lludd and Llefelys* in the Mabinogion, *Beli Mawr,* is a folk memory of this mighty god. His festival was held on 1 May, and the vestigial remains of it lasted into this century in the Highlands with all the essential elements of the pagan feast, modified, of course, by the dictates of Christianity. It was a great period of purification; at this time the Druids, the powerful pagan Celtic priests, used to drive the cattle between two fires, specially kindled, and made of sacred wood, to protect them from disease and the powers of darkness. Human sacrifice and offerings were made, and the ritual would be followed by rejoicing and festivities of all kinds. In recent centuries the sacrifices were replaced by token offerings. Pennant speaks of *Beltain,* or the rural sacrifice, on 1 May. Of Breadalbane he says:

> On the 1st of May, the herdsmen of every village hold their Bel-tein — a rural sacrifice. They cut out a square trench on the

ground, leaving the turf in the middle; on that they make a fire of wood, on which they dress a large caudle of eggs, butter, oatmeal and milk; and bring besides the ingredients of the caudle, plenty of beer and whisky for each of the company must contribute something. The rites begin with spilling some of the caudle on the ground, by way of libation; on that, everyone takes a cake of oatmeal upon which are raised nine square knobs, each dedicated to some particular being, the supposed preserver of their flocks and herds, or to some particular animal, the real destroyer of them; each person then turns his face to the fire, breaks off a knob, and flinging it over his shoulder says 'This I give to thee, *preserve thou my horses;* this to thee, *preserve thou my sheep*' and so on. After that they use the same ceremony to the noxious animals. 'This I give to thee, O Fox! Spare thou my lambs; this to thee O Hooded Crow, this to thee O Eagle.' When the ceremony is over, they dine on the caudle; and after the feast is finished, what is left is hid by two persons deputed for that purpose; but on the next Sunday they re-assemble and finish the reliques of the first entertainment.

And of the Conon region near Dingwall, he says that the sticks placed on the Thursday before Easter over the sheep-cot, the stable or the cow-house were, in his day, carried to the hill on 1 May where the rites were celebrated, all decked with wild flowers, and after the feast was finished, they were replaced on the places from which they had been taken; these sticks were known as *Clou-an-Beltain* or the split branch of the fire of the rock. He goes on to say: 'These follies are now seldom practised, and that with the utmost secrecy; for the Clergy are indefatigable in discouraging every species of superstition.' But in spite of the very considerable power of the Church, the power of time-honoured tradition proved stronger, and these practices persisted into the present century, publicly, or overtly. Shaw, commenting on Moray traditions from the eighteenth century, says that on May Day sacrifices were offered for the preservation of the cattle; the minister stated that, as a boy, he had been present at these. He also used to see, at Mid-summer, the sun-wise procession round the fields with a burning torch of wood, held in the hands of those concerned, in order to obtain a blessing on the corn. On Mid-Summer Eve, fires were kindled near the corn-fields and the people walked round them with burning torches.

Alexander Carmichael has, as always, much important information to give us which he recorded at a time when these pagan ceremonies were still practised to a certain extent, or when those who had taken part in them before they became redundant, were able to give him first-hand information about the details. The first day of May was the day when the summer grazings (*àiridhean*, 'sheilings') began, and there is a whole world of folklore connected with the sheilings alone. The cattle were taken to the hill, together with the sheep and goats; the women and children lived in small bothies and herded the beasts and saw to the dairy produce, and from time to time the men visited them, and there were stories told and songs sung, and the youths courted the girls, and this season was looked upon as the happiest and best of the entire year. After the huts had been repaired a lamb was killed; this was originally a sacrifice, but in Carmichael's time, it was simply eaten as part of the feast at the beginning of the summer grazings at Beltain. The sheilings lasted in Lewis and some other places in the West until well into this century, but the custom, like so many others, has died out. Like everything else in the Celtic world, each activity must be hallowed by ritual; so the Driving of the Cows was sung or incanted for the protection of the beasts on the long journey. Another splendid and heroic mixture of paganism and Christianity is to be found in the incantation *An Saodachadh*, 'The Driving':

> The protection of Odhran the dun be yours,
> The protection of Brigit the Nurse be yours,
> The protection of Mary the Virgin be yours
> In marshes and in rocky ground,
> In marshes and in rocky ground.
>
> The keeping of Ciaran the swart be yours,
> The keeping of Brianan the yellow be yours,
> The keeping of Diarmaid the brown be yours,
> A-sauntering the meadows,
> A-sauntering the meadows.
>
> The safeguard of Fionn mac Cumhall be yours,
> The safeguard of Cormac the shapely be yours,

The safeguard of Conn and Cumhall be yours
From wolf and from bird-flock
From wolf and from bird-flock.

The sanctuary of Colum Cille be yours,
The sanctuary of Maol Ruibhe be yours,
The sanctuary of the milking maid be yours,
To seek you and search for you,
To seek you and search for you.

The encircling of Maol Odhrain be yours,
The encircling of Maol Oighe be yours,
The encircling of Maol Domhnaich be yours,
To protect you and to herd you,
To protect you and to herd you.

The shield of the king of the Fiann be yours
The shield of the king of the sun be yours
The shield of the king of the stars be yours
In jeopardy and distress,
In jeopardy and distress.

The sheltering of the king of kings be yours,
The sheltering of Jesus Christ be yours,
The sheltering of the Spirit of healing be yours,
From evil deed and quarrel,
From evil dog and red dog.

   In this incantation for the protection of the stock we have, once
again, a marvellous blend of pagan characters and Christian saints; a
faith in the elements which were much sworn on by the Celts in
ancient times, and continued to be invoked with equal fervour in a
Christian milieu. Perhaps, in these incantations, recorded for posterity just in time by the devoted labours of Alexander Carmichael,
one can achieve the most profound understanding of the true and
abiding nature of the Celtic psyche and cultural individuality. Just as
the new-born child, or the infant, helpless in its cradle, had need of
every charm and blessing, so must the stock be kept from physical
and supernatural danger by incantation and ritual. Nothing must be
overlooked, nothing left open to the evil forces that constantly lay in
wait to destroy the progeny, the stock, the unwary traveller, the
labouring mother.

Là Beltain, May Day, was then, a most important calendar festival until the end of the nineteenth century. Fires were kindled that day on the mountain tops and all the cattle of the countryside were driven through them to preserve them until next May Day. On this day, all the hearth-fires were extinguished, in order to be kindled from this purifying flame from the sacred fire. In the past, the young people went out to the moors on this day, made a fire, baked a large cake, and this was cut into as many pieces as were people present. One of the pieces was daubed with charcoal and made quite black. Then all the pieces of cake were put into a bonnet, and all the men, who were blindfolded, drew out a piece. The man who selected the blackened piece was doomed to be sacrificed to Belinus; in order to avoid sacrifice, which would, of course, have taken place in pagan times, the victim had to leap six times over the flames. The writer heard of such festivities which still took place in Glen Lyon within living memory.

Lughnasa

Lugh was one of the most widespread and powerful gods both in Europe and in the British Isles. Several towns are named after him, and at Lugudunum (Lyon) an important festival was celebrated on 1 August in honour of the Emperor Augustus and it seems beyond question that this feast replaced one in honour of the native god, whose special day was 1 August. It goes back, then, to pre-Roman times and survived into this century. The Christian Church does not seem to have opposed this festival which was held to mark the *beginning* of the harvest. The feast is, of course, named after the pan-Celtic god, and Cormac in his ninth-century glossary makes the following comments: 'Lughnasa, i.e. the násad of Lugh son of Ethle, i.e. an assembly held by him at the beginning of harvest each year at the coming of Lughnasa.'

Násad means 'games', or 'assembly'; in the Celtic world, the two were synonymous. In modern times, the festival has been called by a variety of different names, masking its pagan connotation, but it is clear that it is the ancient feast which was deeply-embedded in the lives of the people whose well-being depended upon the nature and quality of the year's crops. Originally connected with the corn, it was extended to the potato-harvest as well, when potatoes became the staple diet of the people in Ireland and Scotland. An early Irish tradition has it that Lugh established the festival in honour of his foster-mother, Tailtiu — a close relationship according to Celtic custom. It was a time of much joy, because the people in the Highlands and Islands were very scarce of food before the harvest, and it was essentially a joyous feast, with plenty of good things and treats for all.

Once again, we must look to Carmichael for information in the Highlands and Islands about this festival:

> The day the people began to reap the corn was a day of commotion and ceremonial in the townland. The whole family repaired to the field dressed in their best attire to hail the God of the harvest. Laying his bonnet on the ground, the father of the family took up his sickle, and facing the sun, he cut a handful of corn. Putting the handful of corn three times sunwise round his head, the man raised the 'Iolach Buana' reaping salutation. The whole family took up the strain and praised the God of the harvest, who gave them corn and bread, food and flocks, wool and clothing, health and strength, and peace and plenty. When the reaping was finished the people had a trial called 'cur nan corran', casting the sickles, and 'deuchain chorran', trial of hooks. This consisted, amongst other things, of throwing the sickles high up in the air, and observing how they came down, how each struck the earth, and how it lay on the ground. From these observations the people augured who was to remain single, and who was to be married, who was to be sick and who was to die, before the next reaping came round.

Carmichael recorded a reaping blessing which contains the memory of the agricultural and pagan aspects of the festival.

> On Tuesday of the feast at the rise of the sun,
> And the back of the ear of corn to the east,
> I will go forth with my sickle under my arm,
> And I will reap the cut the first act.
>
> I will let my sickle down,
> While the fruitful ear is in my grasp,
> I will raise mine eye upwards,
> I will turn me on my heel quickly.

> Rightway as travels the sun,
> From the direction of the east to the west,
> From the direction of the north with motion slow,
> To the very core of the direction of the south.
>
> I will give thanks to the king of grace,
> For the growing crops of the ground,
> He will give food to ourselves and to the flocks
> According as He disposeth to us.

The Scottish Lughnasa tradition differed from the Irish and took place on St Michael's Day, 29 September; this would seem to strengthen T. C. Lethbridge's equation of the Christian saint, Michael, with the pagan god, Lugh. This later date is made clear in another incantation recorded by Carmichael:

> The Feast Day of Michael, day beneficent,
> I will put my sickle round about
> The root of my corn as was wont;
> I will lift the first cut quickly,
> I will put it three times round
> My head, saying my rune the while,
> My back to the direction of the north,
> My face to the fair sun of power.
>
> I will throw the handful far from me,
> I will close my two eyes twice,
> Should it fall in one bunch
> My stacks will be productive and lasting,
> No Carlin will come with bad times
> To ask a palm bannock from us,
> What time rough storms come with frowns
> Nor stint nor hardship shall be on us.

Là Féill Moire, 'Feast of St Mary'
Another important day in the Celtic calendar year which was still celebrated in Carmichael's time was *Là Féill Moire*. This took place on 15 August, not long after the traditional Lughnasa feast, which it may have supplanted. Carmichael describes it as follows:

The Feast Day of Mary the Great is the 15th of August. Early in the morning of this day the people go into their fields and pluck ears of corn, generally bere, to make the '*Moilean Moire*'. These ears are laid on a rock exposed to the sun, to dry. When dry, they are husked in the hand, winnowed in a fan, ground in a quern, kneaded on a sheep-skin, and formed into a bannock, which is called '*Moilean Moire*', 'the fatling of Mary'. The bannock is toasted before a fire of rowans or some other sacred wood. Then the husbandman breaks the bannock and gives a bit to his wife and to each of his children, in order according to their ages, and the family raise the '*Iolach Mhoire Mhàthair*' 'The Paean of Mary Mother' who promised to shield them, and who did and will shield them from scath till the day of death. While singing thus, the family walk sunwise round the fire, the father leading, the mother following, and the children following according to age. After going round the fire, the man puts the embers of the fagot-fire, with bits of old iron, into a pot, which he carries sunwise round the outside of his house, sometimes round his steadings and his fields, and his flocks gathered in for the purpose. He is followed without as within by his household, all singing the praise of Mary Mother the while. The scene is striking and picturesque, the family being arrayed in their brightest and singing their best.

> On the feast day of Mary the fragrant,
> Mother of the Shepherd of the flocks,
> I cut me a handful of new corn,
> I dried it gently in the sun,
> I rubbed it sharply from the husk,
> With mine own palms.
>
> I ground it in a quern on Friday,
> I baked it on a fan of sheepskin,
> I toasted it to a fire of rowan,
> And I shared it round my people.
>
> I went sunways round my dwelling
> In the name of Mary Mother,
> Who promised to preserve me,
> Who did preserve me,

And who will preserve me,
In peace, in flocks,
In righteousness of heart,
In labour, in love,
In wisdom, in mercy,
For the sake of Thy Passion.
Thou Christ of grace
Who till the day of my death
Wilt never forsake me!
Oh, till the day of my death
Wilt never forsake me.

Maire MacNeill, in her brilliant book, *The Festival of Lughnasa,* deals mainly with the Irish evidence; she rightly comments, of the Scottish surviving traditions, on the gravity and formality with which they were performed, in contrast to the 'rustic high spirits' of the Irish assemblies.

The end of the harvest was also marked by feasting and dancing and celebrations of all kinds. There are still many traditions extant about the cutting of the Corn Dolly or Maiden, '*A'Mhaighdean*' as

Corn dollies

the last sheaf was widely named in the Highlands. It is still done in parts of the Highlands, and the writer has been in farmhouses in central Perthshire where the Maiden occupies a prominent place in the kitchen, waiting for the first day of ploughing, when it is traditionally given to the horses. In this mechanised age, the cows often get the Corn Dolly instead. This custom was once widespread in Britain; the last sheaf was regarded as a symbol of good luck and treated with great respect and honour. Sometimes it was placed in the local Church; at other times it decorated the farmer's house. Now that the conviviality and communal spirit of the harvest field have given way to the solitary efficiency of mechanical harvesters it is a custom that has almost died out as a spontaneous folk practice. In the Highlands, apart from the few places where the tradition survives vestigially, details can still be obtained from the local people about what really went on when the custom was universal. Even in the small area of Loch Tayside and the Carse of Dull in Perthshire, the custom varied from farm to farm. And over the entire Highland area there were marked variations in practice. One important detail was in the identity of the person who was to actually scythe the Maiden. In Rannoch, it was the youngest person on the harvest-field who cut the last sheaf; this could be either a girl or a boy. The writer met one man who remembers cutting it as a boy on Loch Tayside, and the great honour that was accorded to him on that occasion. No doubt in pagan times, a maiden was actually sacrificed after being decked and carried round the fields, and her blood would be a means of ensuring a successful harvest in the following year. This custom is ancient, and in Gaul the image of a goddess used to be carried round the fields with great ritual and solemnity.

In Strathtay it was the farmer himself who cut the Maiden and this tradition continued into recent times, but it was not followed by any special celebration; in Glenlochay, it was likewise the farmer who cut the last sheaf. Near Kenmore, Perthshire, the Maiden was given to the horses when the first load of the next year's harvest was brought in. A native of Glenlyon remembers how universal this practice was when she was a girl. She still carries it on in her own farm, and the Maiden is given to the horses on the first day of ploughing. In Glen Lyon the last sheaf was called *A'Mhaighdean*, and dressed like a young girl if the harvest was a good one; if bad, it was called the *Cailleach*, 'Hag', and dressed up like an old woman. This is the typical Celtic concept of the duality of the goddess — young, beautiful, favourable to mankind, or old, hideous, and hostile. In Skye, Harris and in Kintail one of the names for the last sheaf was the *Gobhar Bhacach*, 'Lame Goat'; it is interesting to note that at Saint Gall (Switzerland) the last sheaf was known as the 'Crooked Goat'. In the Hebrides and other areas, the last sheaf had rather sinister associations. It was used as a dire insult to the man who was last in cutting his corn. This could result in actual physical violence and bloodshed, and would seem to be reminiscent of some ancient ritual connected with harvest sacrifice, for which there is plenty of evidence in the pagan Celtic world, as we have noted above. A man who had cut his own *Cailleach* or *Gobhar Bhacach* could throw it into the field of a farmer who was still working on his grain. It was considered very unlucky to be the last person in the community to finish the harvest. Anyone receiving the last sheaf in this manner regarded it as a very bad omen, because it was widely-believed that he would have to support an actual *Cailleach* throughout the winter. There are accounts dating to the last century of the violence done to those who were caught by a farmer throwing the last sheaf onto his land; in one instance the messenger was 'caught, stripped, clipped, and sent home naked'. This was one of the lighter penalties for such an act. One cannot wonder at this because it was firmly believed that:

> Loss of cattle, loss on account of death and accident
> Will befall the luckless one of the Gobhar Bhacach.

As a result of this belief, no one wanted to be last with his corn-cutting and there was tremendous activity in order to complete the work in good time. It was customary in the Hebrides to bind up the straw, the last sheaf of corn cut on the field and to fashion it into the likeness of a woman with dock leaves, stalks of ragwort and all tied into shape with many-coloured threads. In Argyll, Uist, parts of Perthshire, etc., this was known as the Cailleach, as we have seen. A special ritual was observed when someone wanted to insult a neighbour by throwing the Cailleach or Maiden into his field; usually, a young man hastily mounted his horse and galloped at full speed past the uncut field of his neighbour, pretending he was going somewhere else; he would then fling the Cailleach into the field as he passed. The punishments varied as we have seen, if the offender was caught, and one of these was known as *bearradh eòin is amadain air*, 'a clipping of bird and of a fool on him'; this meant the shaving off of the culprit's beard and hair. People felt so strongly about this insult and the hazards it would bring to the household that a crofter would seemingly prefer to see his best cow drop dead than have the Cailleach thrown into his fields.

Là Fèill Bharr, 'Feast of St Barr'

Martin Martin records that all the inhabitants of Barra observed the Festival of Saint Barr, the patron saint of the island on 27 September. It was their custom to ride on horseback, and this ritual ride was concluded by riding three times round St Barr's Church. Martin tells how a foreign priest happened to arrive on the island while this festival was in progress. The inhabitants immediately asked him to preach a commemoration service in honour of their patron, St Barr, according to ancient custom. The priest had never even heard of St Barr 'and knowing nothing of his virtues could say nothing in his praise'. He did, however, offer to preach about St Paul or St Peter; this greatly upset the natives. They said he could not be a true priest if he had not heard of St Barr for the Pope himself was aware of him. Priest and people parted with mutual ill-feeling. They also had another cavalcade on St Michael's Day, two days later. All strangers, together with the family must eat bread that night, according to Martin.

'St Michael's Day'

Michael was an immensely popular Highland saint, and was indeed invoked widely throughout the Celtic world. As we have seen, he would appear to have taken over the role of some earlier pagan protector, as was so often the case. Michael was indeed spoken of as 'the god Michael' right down to Carmichael's time, and *brian* Michael. Brian, together with his brothers Iuchar and Iucharba, was one of the three chief gods of pagan Ireland, sons of Danu, the great mother goddess. An incantation, recorded again by Carmichael, in honour of the saint, makes a frank equation between him and his pagan predecessor.

> You were the warrior of courage
> Going on the journey of prophecy,
> You would not travel on a cripple,
> You did take the steed of the god Michael,
> He was without bit in his mouth,
> You did ride him on the wing,
> You did leap over the knowledge of nature.

These lines would not have been out of place in any description of a typical Celtic deity riding his unbridled horse fearlessly through the skies, or over the seas.

This feast which must have a great antiquity in the Highlands is frequently referred to by Martin Martin. Of Lewis, he says that all the inhabitants were Protestant, apart from one Catholic family; at Michaelmas they had a cavalcade and both sexes rode on horse-back. There was a cavalcade on the island of Coll on St Michael's Day. He gives a dramatic account of some riders he encountered when he came from South Uist. He saw some 60 men riding along the sands, directing their course for the east sea 'and being between me and the sun, they made a great figure on the plain sands; we discovered them to be natives of South Uist for they alighted from their horses and went to gather cockles in the sands which are exceedingly plentiful there'. He states that there was a general cavalcade there on All Saints Day; the people baked the St Michael's Cake at night, and the family and any strangers present ate it together at supper. Of Hirt (St Kilda) Martin records that on the Festival of All Saints the natives baked a large cake in the form of a triangle, furrowed round, and it must all be eaten that night. The people were extremely hospitable to strangers. There were 18 horses on the island in Martin's time; the inhabitants used to ride them at the Anniversary Cavalcade of All Saints; this feast they never failed to observe. They used to begin at the shore and ride as far as the houses. The only harness used was a straw rope to control the horse's head. Of Harris, Martin says the people observed St Michael's Day (all the inhabitants were Protestant) when they came together on horse-back and made their cavalcade on the sands at low water.

Martin has some interesting details about St Michael's Day customs in North Uist as he himself witnessed them. He says that the natives were much given to horse-riding, and they kept St Michael's Day, both sexes then riding on horse-back. The meeting-place was a large stretch of firm sand on the shore, and there they held horse races for small prizes, and these were eagerly sought after. He mentions an ancient custom whereby it was considered to be lawful for any of the inhabitants to steal his neighbour's horse the night before the race and ride him all next day, provided he deliver him safe to the owner after the race. He describes the manner of racing; a race consisted of a few young men using neither saddles nor bridles, only two small ropes made of bent in place of a bridle; they had no spurs, using only their bare heels. And when they began the race, they threw these ropes on their horses' necks and drove them vigorously with a piece of long seaware in each hand instead of a whip. This had been dried in the sun for several months before the Festival. As the people only met together on Sundays, such calendar festivals were regarded as times of great relaxation and joy. The men used to ride with their sweethearts behind them on horseback and gave each other presents. The men traditionally gave the women knives and purses; the women gave the men a pair of fine carrots.

Carmichael, as always, has invaluable details to add to our knowledge of this much-loved saint and his festival. Michael was the patron saint of the sea; and various islands off the coasts of Britain, and Mont-Saint-Michel in Brittany, further testify to the connection of the saint both with eminences and the sea. He was also the patron saint of coastal districts, boats, horses and horsemen – hence the emphasis on horse-racing at his feast. Horse-racing was likewise a main feature of the ancient pagan *Lughnasa* Festival in Ireland, this perhaps strengthening the link between the god Lugh and the 'god' Michael. Temples were dedicated to him on the coasts in the Celtic countries; the late T. C. Lethbridge noted the close connection between Iron Age hill-forts and dedications to Michael. Thus the Festival of St Michael on 29 September was, perhaps, one of the most blatantly pagan feasts of the Christian calendar, although the old faith was never far beneath the surface of any. On St Michael's Eve, carrots were brought in, a special bannock called the *struan* was baked, lambs were sacrificed, and horses were stolen. On the Day, there was a special early Mass, and the lamb and the cake were distributed; then there was a pilgrimage to the local burial-ground in honour of the ancestors — also an ancient pagan practice, worship of the ancestors and propitiation of the dead. There was a service at the burial-ground and a circuit of the churchyard was made. Carrots were then exchanged, and wishes were made during this act. The *oda* took place when horses were raced and athletic sports were indulged in. The Festival, in fact, much resembled the Old Irish descriptions of the feasts held under the aegis of the god and king. With night came revelry and merry-making of every kind. It was regarded as an auspicious time for love-making and betrothal. One person was appointed to guard the crops on St Michael's Day and to make a circuit of the township on St Michael's Night. Some days before the Festival, the women and girls gathered wild carrots. This was usually on the afternoon of the Sunday before the Feast and it was called *Dòmhnach Curran,* 'Carrot Sunday'. If the soil was moist the carrots could be pulled out easily. If not, a special small three-pronged mattock was used; each woman would sing an incantation while pulling the sacred carrots. Carmichael records one of these chants which he heard from an old woman who had gathered carrots eighty years ago:

> Cleft, fruitful, fruitful, fruitful,
> Joy of carrots surpassing upon me,
> Michael the brave endowing me,
> Bride the fair be aiding me.
>
> Progeny pre-eminent over every progeny,
> Progeny on my womb,
> Progeny pre-eminent over every progeny,
> Progeny on my progeny.

To find a forked carrot was regarded as remarkably good luck and to be symbolic of real fertility. The women try to rival each other in getting the most and best carrots. A special bag was suspended from the waist to put the culled carrots in, and this was known as a *crioslachan*, 'little girdle'. The carrots are washed and tied up in small bunches of red thread; they were then put in pits near the houses and covered with sand. The people used to work all through the night on St Michael's Eve. The men guarded their horses and stables, for people would try to steal a horse to use on the circuits of the following day. One proverb says:

> Theft of horse on the Feast of Michael,
> Theft that never was condemned.

It was essential to leave one horse for each man, but it could be the poorest of beasts. After the festivities, the horse must be returned to its owner. A male lamb without blemish was sacrificed and known as *Uan Mìcheil*, 'the Michael Lamb'. The cake was made from all the cereals grown on the land during the year and the meal was used in equal parts in the *struan*, 'bannock'. It was baked on a lamb-skin and moistened with sheep's milk. For this reason, the ewes were kept in milk until after 29 September and then allowed to go dry. The eldest daughter of the house baked the *struan* with her mother's assistance. A special stone was brought from the moor by the boys, and known as the *leac struain* 'struan slab', and it was placed on edge by the fire and the bannock then set on edge before it. The fire was made up of sacred woods — oak, rowan, bramble. The making of the Michael bannock was a complicated operation; three layers of a batter consisting of cream, eggs and butter were laid on each side alternately. It was essential that the *struan* should not break while it was in the process of being cooked. If the stone on which the cake rested fell over, taking the cake with it, this was regarded as an evil omen to the whole family. No one would use a *struan* that had been broken. All the families would take their *struan* to Church on St Michael's Day to have them blessed. After Mass, the people ate the Michael Day feast in their homes, the man of the house carving the lamb and dividing the bannock. The whole family would stand round, holding a piece of the cake and praising Michael. Any remaining lamb and cake were then given to the poor. In fact, on that sacred day it was the custom for each family to make a generous offering of goods of all kinds to those less fortunate than themselves.

After the distribution of the food, the families would mount their horses and set out to make a circuit of St Michael's burial ground. Husband and wife customarily rode on one horse; the children were also somehow fitted in as well. The priest would lead the procession, wearing a white robe and riding on a white horse; it must have been a magnificent sight to witness. If there was more than one priest present, they would ride abreast. While the circuit was being made all the people would sing the *Iolach Mìcheil*, Song of Michael the Victorious. After this ceremony, each girl presented her lover with a handful of carrots. Then the *oda* began. According to Carmichael's information, the men raced their horses bare-headed, wearing only short trews and a shirt, without saddle or bridle. Sometimes the girls would compete with one another, sometimes with the men. The girls likewise rode bareback. Circuiting of some kind continued througout the day. St. Michael's night was a time for high revelry in every township. The chief piper had the honour of selecting the place for the *Céilidh*, 'party'. If the piper was a married man, each man present would make him some contribution; if single, he would play for no recompense. Fiddlers and other musicians also augmented the piping throughout the joyous night. It was the custom of the women to put their carrots into a linen bag with the name of the owner. During the day and the evening celebrations gifts were exchanged between the sexes.

Special dances and scenes were enacted on St Michael's Night which show clearly the pagan origin of the Festival. One of these was a dance called *Cailleach an Dùdain*, 'the Hag of the Mill-dust'. Carmichael himself saw it performed many times; it was danced by a man and a woman. The man held a rod in his right hand known as the *Slachdan Druidheachd*, 'the Druid Wand' or the *Slachdan Geasachd*, 'the Magic Wand'. The man would hold the wand over his own head and then over the head of the woman. She then would fall down at his feet, as if dead. He then mourns for her, dancing about her body. Then he would raise her left hand, touch it with the wand and the hand would come to life and begin to move up and down. The man is overjoyed, and he would then dance about her. Next he would bring her other arm and her legs to life. Then he would kneel over her and breathe into her mouth and touch her heart with the wand. This would restore her fully to life, she would spring to her feet, and both would dance joyously. The music changed with the different stages of this curious performance. The instrument might be the pipes, the fiddle or even *port-a-beul*, 'mouth music' which was often used at *céilidhs* instead of a musical instrument. According to Carmichael the accompanying music is peculiar and irregular and the words archaic. It seems beyond question that this dance is related to the kind of cult scenes that were mimed at the ancient pagan festivals in the wider Celtic world and have long lingered on its periphery. The great collector, Iain F.

Campbell of Islay also witnessed the dancing of *Cailleach an Dudain*. Another strange dance, *Cath nan Coileach*, 'The Battle of the Cocks', and *Ruidhleadh nan Coileach Dubha*, 'The Reel of the Black Cocks', were danced on St Michael's Night, as was the sword dance, another primitive and pagan dance; on that night, however, it was danced in eight sections instead of four. That this triumphal dance over the weapon goes directly back to pagan times is evidenced by its depiction on certain Gaulish coins dating to the pre-Roman period.

All night long, individual *struans* were given and received. People of all ranks joined together in this ceremony. By the time Carmichael was collecting in the Highlands, this rich tradition had become obsolete, but memories and tales of it still survive. The last traditional circuiting of St Michael's burial-ground in South Uist seemingly took place in 1820; the last great *oda* in North Uist was in 1866 and took place on the Strand of Mary, on the west side of the island. Vestigially, the Michael lamb continued to be slain, the *struan* baked and the carrots picked, but by people who had no real understanding of the earlier significance of these things. Carmichael perspicaciously remarks, of affairs in his own day:

> In the present, as a rule, the proprietors and gentlemen of the Highlands and Islands are at the best but temporary residents, if so much, and generally strangers in blood and speech, feeling and sympathy, more prone to criticize than to help, to scoff than to sympathize. As a result, the observances of the people have fallen into disuse, to the loss of the spiritual life of the country, and of the patriotic life of the nation.

Michael was, according to tradition, the leader of souls to the next world, just as was Mercury according to classical tradition; and it is not without interest that Lugh was clearly a kind of Celtic Mercury, enticing humans to his home in the Otherworld.

Samhain, 'Hallowe'en'

Hallowe'en, from the earliest Celtic records, has been the most important and sinister festival of the Celtic year. It was originally celebrated on the night of 1 November and on the following day. Then the whole world was believed to be infested by the gods and spirits of the pagan Celts, and the Otherworld became visible to, and accessible to mankind. The occupants of the supernatural world could mix freely, a privilege fraught with peril for human beings. Originally a Druidic festival, and accompanied as the Irish tales indicate, with human sacrifice and many propitiatory offerings, it remained the most popular of the calendar festivals, and was celebrated with much ritual well into this century. It is still observed vestigially, but the old significance has been lost. Different parts of the Highlands still carry on their own traditional activities, but these are less authentic and varied as the old beliefs and traditional ways of celebrating rapidly disappear. Divining the future by means of nuts, kail plants, dropping egg whites into water and so on, was a regular pursuit, and sometimes the person seeking to know the future would get unexpected and perhaps unwanted answers to the questions asked. The supernatural would really manifest itself, or one of the company would play a trick and make the seeker after future knowledge believe that this was the case. In many districts each house had its own bonfire, *samhnag,* and one house was usually especially popular as a gathering place. In early Celtic tradition, *Samhain* was closely associated with the burial mounds which were believed to be some of the entrances to the Otherworld; and for this reason, the celebration of Hallowe'en at Fortingall, at the head of Glenlyon in Perthshire, is of especial interest.

The festival itself was observed in a somewhat unusual fashion, being essentially of a communal nature there, apart from anything else, and it continued well into this century. Another unusual feature in this region of the Highlands where so much archaic tradition has been preserved, was the date on which the festival was traditionally held – 11 November. The *samhnag,* 'bonfire', was a communal effort, and it was built on the mound known as *Càrn nam Marbh,* 'The Mound of the Dead'. Local tradition has it that the mound contains the bodies of victims of a dreadful plague which were brought there and buried by an old woman with a cart or sled pulled by a white horse; the story has a clear supernatural flavour about it, and the mound is, in fact, a Bronze Age tumulus. A stone, known as *Clach a' Phlàigh,* 'the Plague Stone' crowns the mound. Although people living in the neighbourhood knew of the Fortingall ceremonies, only the local populace seems to have taken part in them. In the other townships the usual individual bonfires were lit, and it was usually the children who built them.

The following account was obtained from a local man who actually took part in the celebrations as a boy. Everybody shared in the preparations which began months before the event. The young people used to go up onto the hill to collect and store great quantities of whin, which was once very plentiful there. This went on night after night. It was finally made into a huge pile with wood shavings and tar barrels added to increase the great conflagration. It was the duty of the older men to actually build the bonfire on the top of the Mound of the Dead. Finally, it was lit, and the whole community took hands when it was blazing and danced round the mound both sunwise and anti-sunwise. As the fire began to wane, some of the younger boys took burning faggots from the flames and ran throughout the field with them, finally throwing them into the air and dancing over them as they lay glowing on the ground. When the last embers were showing, the boys would have a leaping competition across the remains of the fire. When it was finished, the young people went home and ducked for apples and practised divination. The older people went to Fortingall Hotel, an old coaching house, and held a dance there, with much merry-making. There was no 'guising' here, the bonfire being the absolute centre of attention until it was consumed. The last bonfire, made by the community, was lit on the mound in 1924. It is said that this ancient festival was finally destroyed, not only because interest in such things was dying out amongst the young, nor because the people ceased to remember it, but because it was stopped by the keeper who claimed that this great stripping of cover from the hill was interfering with the game there. It is thought locally that the unusual date of *Samhain* here was due to the fact that the date of the big Fortingall *Féill* or Market was held then, and there was some association between the two gatherings. In other places, the ceremony was observed on the traditional date and the activities varied from region to region.

After sunset, in many places, every youth who was able to carry a blazing torch or *Samhnag* ran out and circuited the boundaries of their farms with these blazing brands in order to protect the family possessions from the fairies and all malevolent forces. Then, having secured their homes in this manner, by the purifying force of the sacred fire, all the households in a township would gather together and participate in the traditional activities. Nuts and apples were regularly used. In the Hebrides the boys dressed up as guisers and went from house to house; much damage to property was done by them on this wild night, gates being removed, carts overturned, and mischief of every kind indulged in. One means of divining the future was to place six plates on the floor, each with different contents. The girls of the house were blindfolded and led to the spot where the plates were laid down, and the first plate each blindfolded girl touched foretold her fate. Pennant likewise makes mention of these widespread Hallowe'en customs. He says that in his day the young people determine the figure and size of their husbands by drawing cabbages blindfold; and to divine the future, fling nuts into the fire.

When the festival was carried out with complete solemnity, new fire, kindled from the sacred communal fire was brought into each house at Samhain, and it is likely that, like the Beltain fires, the *Samain* fire was made from *tein-éigin,* fire made from the friction of two pieces of wood. Stones were sometimes placed in the great fire for purposes of divination. Traces of the original orgiastic nature of the festival remained in the Highlands until the end of the last century at least. In origin, *Samain* was clearly a pastoral festival, held to assist the powers of growth and fertility, to placate the dead and keep at bay the forces of evil, to please the gods (and later certain saints who had replaced them) with sacrifice, and as a clear demarcation between the joys of the ingathered harvest, and the hardships of the approaching winter.

These calendar festivals, then, not only provided occasions for religious and superstitious ritual, when the protection of the gods and, later, God and the saints was sought against the countless hostile powers; they were times of great relaxation and feasting, games and entertainment of every kind, in a society which lived in many cases very near to subsistence level, and daily life consisted of heavy toil and labour and utter dependence on the elements and their influence on crop and stock, and the vital harvest of the sea.

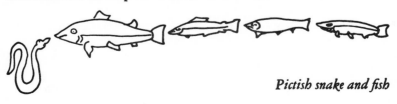

Pictish snake and fish

Netherton head

Epilogue

IN THIS book, the first of three on the folklore of the Scottish Highlands, the emphasis has been laid on those aspects of the vast and rich tradition which are essentially Celtic, and have a long ancestry in the Celtic world. Many topics have had to be omitted, due to the dictates of length, but these will feature in future volumes. They include not only the vast repertoire of tales, heroic and humorous, which so delight the Highland mind, but countless legends of birds and beasts; sacred springs and severed heads; holy trees and magic mounds; dread supernatural beings that were believed to populate the lonely moors and mountains; fairies; hags; water monsters — black dogs, evil aggressive goats, sinister and dangerous bulls. In fact, the amount of recorded material of every kind is almost unbelievably large and varied, some published, much awaiting publication in the Archives of the School of Scottish Studies and elsewhere. I have used published material in many instances, but only when I have been able to corroborate the evidence by personal field collection and ascertain that practices and

155

beliefs previously recorded are, in fact, valid.

The richness and the sophistication of Highland folklore and legend are due, partly, to the fact that so much of it has been handed on by means of the oral tradition which was so highly developed in Celtic societies from earliest times. It is also a manifestation of the spirit of the Gaels themselves; their love of words, their deep involvement with nature and the beauties of nature, and their intense passion for immediate locality, their homeland. The songs and poems of exile reveal in a deeply moving way this aspect of the Celtic psyche. Thus the songs and poems, the hero tales, legends of fairies, ghosts and monsters and a nostalgic preoccupation with the past, provided the sole relaxation in lives which were spent in the relentless struggle to obtain a sufficiency of food and clothing and shelter which was the daily lot of the crofters and cottars of the Highlands in past times. Nevertheless, the Celthas always had a great capacity for joy. He has always faced his rigorous life cheerfully and without complaint, his active mind and deep enjoyment of his home, his language and his rich store-house of traditions doing much to compensate for paucity of worldy goods or entertainment of a more sophisticated kind. All is now, of course, changing. Radio and television, improved communications, higher standards of living and the opening up of the west to tourists have all played a vital role in transforming much that survived until the middle of this century; and it has not yet entirely gone. There is still a surprisingly large body of tradition to be heard and collected while the older people who knew a different way of life remain to give testimony to the past. But whatever survives in the way of superstitious belief — for superstition dies hard in every human milieu — the situation described to the great collector J. F. Campbell of Islay, by Hector Urquhart, gamekeeper at Ardkinglas, will never return. He says:

In my native place, Pool-ewe, Ross-shire, when I was a boy, it was the custom for the young to assemble together on the long winter nights to hear the old people recite the tales or *sgeulachd*, which they had learned from their fathers before them. In these days tailors and shoemakers went from house to house making our clothes and shoes. When one of them came to the village we were greatly delighted, whilst getting new kilts at the same time.

I knew an old tailor who used to tell a new tale every night during his stay in the village; and another, an old shoe-maker, who, with his large stock of stories about ghosts and fairies, used to frighten us so much that we scarcely dared pass the neighbouring churchyard on our way home . . . it was a common saying 'the first tale by the goodman, and tales to daylight by the guest'.

Rather than lament the rich treasure-house of lore and legend that has been irretrievably lost down the centuries, we should be deeply grateful at the amount of invaluable oral material that has been saved for posterity by the tireless labours and utter devotion of dedicated collectors, past and present.

Notes

(Martin Martin's *A Description of the Western Islands of Scotland* is so consistently concerned with the folklife of the people that it has not been thought necessary to give page numbers in the following notes to the very numerous references to this book. Readers are recommended to study the book, which was first published in London in 1703 and republished, edited by D J Macleod, by Eneas Mackay of Stirling in 1934.)

1 *Introduction,* pages 11-22
The quotation on page 11 is from Grant, D., 1956, 202.
SOUTH CADBURY: Alcock, 1972.
ANCESTORS AND GRAVES: for obsession with the veneration of ancestors and the cult of graves in early times see Caesar, *Gallic War,* VI, 18; for a full discussion of this see MacCulloch, 1911, 333-47.
LINEAGE: the pagan Celts usually traced their lineage back to a king, divinised monarch or god; for example, see MacCulloch, 1911, 333-47; Tierney, 1960, 273; Ross, 1970, 64 f.
BAGPIPES: Collinson, 1966, 159-98, traces the origin and development of bagpipes and their music in Scotland; Collinson, 1975, expands these studies.
EARLY CELTIC ART: the most recent and comprehensive study of form and design in European and insular Early Celtic Art, with superb illustrations, is to be found in Megaw, 1970. The UNESCO *Courier* for December 1975 is devoted entirely to magnificently illustrated articles on various aspects of the Early Celtic world.
FIONN: stories of Fionn Mac Cumhaill and his followers in early Celtic tradition and later folklore are found in many early and late sources including Campbell, J. F., 1862, who discusses the Ossianic controversy in detail; O'Grady, 1892; Thomson, 1952, who brings the discussion up to date with a full bibliography; Murphy, 1953; Cross and Slover, 1969.
OGMIOS: the Celtic god of eloquence; Ross, 1967, 381.
ORAL TRADITION: for references to this among the early Celts in

Caesar, *Gallic War,* VI, 14, see Tierney, 1960, 272.
GAELIC LABOUR SONGS: Collinson, 1966, 67-117.
COLUMBA: 'Thursday the day of the kindly Columba'; Carmichael, 1928, I, 163.
LUGHNASA: MacNeill, 1962, *passim*; the interesting suggestion is made that the Lammas Fairs and Puck Fairs were in fact survivals of the ancient Celtic Lughnasa Festival.
SAMHUIN (Hallowe'en): Ross, 1967, 23 *et al.*
HIGHLAND REBELLION, 1745-46: Prebble, 1961.
HIGHLAND EVICTIONS: Prebble, 1963.
JOHN CARSWELL: MacKechnie, 1964.
BOOK OF INVASIONS: Cross and Slover, 1969, 3, *Leabhar Gabhála Eireann,* The Book of the Takings of Ireland.
OSSIAN: for discussions of the Ossianic controversy see FIONN *supra.*

2 *Clan Lore,* pages 23-32
DRESS: a representative example of protective dress can be seen in the burial ground of the parish church at Glenorchy, Dalmally, Lorn, Argyll, on a slab with the effigy of an armed man wearing a tall helmet (bascinet) and a shirt of mail (akteon or acton); *R.C.A.H.M.S.,* 1974, No. 246 (2), p 21.
LEGENDS: clan legends still circulate in the Scottish Highlands; MacKechnie, 1964.
HISTORY: Many collections of Gaelic tales contain clan legends and historical episodes; for an example of the history of one important clan see Grant, I.F., 1959.

3 *Seers and Second Sight,* pages 33-62
THE GHOST: Grant, D, 1956, 68.
SEERS: for seers in early Celtic society (Latin *vates,* Old Irish *filed,* Welsh *gweledd*) see Tierney, 1960, 269, quoting Strabo.
SECOND SIGHT: for Dr Samuel Johnson and second sight, see Boswell, 1941, 123 f.: for how Fionn obtained his power of 'the Sight', Cross and Slover, 1969, 365: see also Campbell, J. G., 1902, 120 f.
DROWNING: for further examples of seers and drowning see Campbell, J. G., 1902, 160 f.
DEATH AND ANCESTORS: for further discussion of this cult see

MacCulloch, 1911, 165 f.

BEATINGS: for near-fatal beatings by a deity in ancient Celtic belief see, for example, Cross and Slover, 1969, 179 f.

BROWNIE: *gruagach,* a supernatural being who watched over the herds or became attached to a particular household where it did menial tasks about the house. A full description of this creature is given in Carmichael, 1928, II, 306 f.

FRITH MHOIRE: Carmichael, 1954, 287.

OBA NAM BUADH: Carmichael, 1928, I, 6 f.

BAN-SHEE: *bean-sidhe* was a female spirit who used to attach herself to some individual family and could be heard wailing if a death in the family was imminent; she could be dangerous if offended.

GLAISTIG: a malevolent water-sprite, half goat, half female, who haunted remote waters to the danger of travellers.

BAN-NIGH: a supernatural washer-woman who haunted fords and river sides, washing the shrouds of those about to die and singing a dirge. If she could be surprised and seized she would grant three wishes to her captor in return for her freedom.

FUATH: a monster haunting glens and waters, much feared by mankind.

URUISG: a water monster, part goat and part human, with long, unkempt hair.

ORA CEARTAIS: Carmichael, 1941, 145.

BULL-HIDES: for ritual see Piggott, 1962.

4 *Witchcraft, Black and White,* pages 63-91

THE CHARM OF MARY: Carmichael, 1941, 151 f.

WITCH OF LAGGAN: MacPherson, 1893, 23 f.

MACLEAN OF DUART: for the story of MacLean and the clay image, see Campbell, J. G., 1902, 47.

ROWAN TREE COLLAR: Campbell, J. G., 1902, 12.

'IT IS MY OWN EYE': Carmichael, A., 1941, 157.

BRIGIT: Carmichael, A., 1941, 51.

SEVERED HEADS AND WELLS: Ross, 1967, 61-127.

EPILEPSY: Carmichael, A., 1941, 268-69.

CHILD BORN FULLY GROWN: Jones and Jones, 1973, 30.

AILEIN NAN SOP: Campbell, J. G., 1902, 45 f.

'FOUR TO WORK SICKNESS': Carmichael, A., 1941, 151.

EVIL EYE: Carmichael, A., 1941, 151 f.

'THY STRAIT...': Carmichael, A., 1941, 92.

'IT IS MINE OWN EYE': Carmichael, A., 1941, 157.

'I AM LIFTING...': Carmichael, A., 1941, 93.

'SHAKE FROM THEE...': Carmichael, A., 1941, 94.

THREADS: for this charm see Carmichael, A., 1941, 166 f.

HEALING: Carmichael, A., 1941, 167 f.

BALOR AND HIS EVIL EYE: Cross and Slover, 1969, 44.

5 *Cures, Omens, Tabus and Social Customs,* pages 92-106.

HERBAL CURES IN ANTIQUITY: see Pliny the Elder (AD 23-79), *Nat. His.* XVI, XCV; XXIV 103 f.

KING'S EVIL, SCROFULA: chronic enlargement and degeneration of lymphatic glands. Famous Highland physicians: for Beatons in Skye see Grant I.F., 1959, 162 f.

LUCKY DAYS AND UNLUCKY DAYS: for one example of the reading of omens by the Druid Cathbad, father of the Ulster King Conchobor Mac Nessa at the turn of the Christian era, see O'Rahilly, 1967, 163.

LUCKY AND UNLUCKY SIGNS: Carmichael, 1954, 288 f.

HUMAN SACRIFICE: Ross, 1967, 19-23 *et. al.*

FOUNDATION SACRIFICE: for one version of the sacrifice of Odhran see Adamnan's *Life of Saint Columba* edited by Reeve, 288.

ISLAND OF WOMEN: one example of an island inhabited in antiquity entirely by women, situated off the mouth of the river Loire is mentioned by Strabo, IV, 6 (Tierney, 1960, 269).

CELTIC HOSPITALITY: in antiquity, see Diodorus the Sicilian, V, 5 (Tierney, 1960, 250).

POWER OF SATIRE: for bards as eulogists and satirists in pagan Gaulish society see Diodorus the Sicilian, V, 31 (Tierney, 1960, 251).

'WITH ITS BACK ...': for a variant of this verse see Carmichael, 1928, I, 185.

6 *Life and Death,* pages 107-116

DEATH RITES: Pennant, 1769, I, 98.

BEAN-TUIRM: Carmichael, 1954, 339 f.: Pliny implies that such women were known in Britain before the 1st century AD: *Nat. Hist.,* XXII, 295.

MIDWIFE AND MOURNING WOMAN: Carmichael, 1954, 345.

7 *The Seasons: Calendar Festivals and the Daily Round,* pages 117-154

CHRISTMAS: Carmichael, 1928, I, 127 f.

HOGMANAY: Carmichael, 1928, I, 149 f.

TREATMENT OF CATTLE: Pennant, 1769, I, 186.

SMOORING THE FIRE: Carmichael, 1928, I, 237 f.

BRIGIT: for details of her pagan role see Ross, 1967, 206.

BRIDE: for the genealogy, see Carmichael, 1928, I, 164 f.

RITES ASSOCIATED WITH BRIDE'S DAY: Carmichael, 1928, I, 164, f.

'EARLY ON BRIDE'S MORN': Carmichael, 1928, I, 169 f.

LUGHNASA: in the Irish Lughnasa Festivals a great hostile snake was believed to live in a hole close to many of the sites where the assemblies were traditionally held: MacNeill, 1962.

SACRIFICIAL DEATH: Lucan makes reference to sacrificial death by burning, stabbing and drowning to three powerful gods of the pagan Celtic world: Ross, 1967, 248.

HEBRIDEAN OFFERINGS: for reference to sacrificial offerings to a sea-god in the Hebrides see Carmichael, 1928, I, 163. The writer has met people in the Outer Hebrides who remember this custom taking place in their childhood. Traditions have also been collected from natives of Lewis living in Southampton

'THURSDAY OF COLUMBA BENIGN': Carmichael, 1928, I, 163.

LLUDD A LEFELYS: for this story in the *Mabinogion* see Jones and Jones, 1973, 89-94.

AN SAODACHADH: 'The Driving', Carmichael, 1941, 43.

LUGHNASA ASSEMBLY: for the origin of this see MacNeill, 1962, chapter 1: for Cormac in this context see MacNeill, 1962, 3.

LUGHNASA ACTIVITIES: Carmichael, 1928, I, 246 f.

LUGH EQUATED WITH MICHAEL: Lethbridge, 1962, 50.

LA FEILL MOIRE: Carmichael, 1928, I, 194 f.

FERTILITY GODDESSES: for the Gaulish custom of carrying the image of a fertility goddess round the fields, see MacCulloch, 1911, 92.

CAILLEACH: Carmichael, 1941, 37 f.

ST MICHAEL'S DAY: Lethbridge, 1962, 47 *et al.:* Carmichael, 1928, I, 190 f.

CROOKED GOAT: Frazer, 1920, 281 f.

Epilogue, pages 155-157.

HECTOR URQUHART: Campbell, J. F., 1860, xiv-xv.

Folk and Clan Museums

Am Fasgadh, Kingussie, Inverness-shire
Angus Folk Museum, Glamis, Angus
Auchindrain Museum, Inveraray, Argyll
Clan Donnachaidh Museum, Calvine, Blair Atholl, Perthshire
Clan Macpherson Museum, Newtonmore, Inverness-shire
Broughty Castle Museum, Dundee
Fife Folk Museum, Ceres, Cupar, Fife
Gladstone Court Street Museum, Biggar, Lanarkshire
Old Glasgow Museum, Glasgow Green, Glasgow
Glencoe and North Lorn Folk Museum, Glencoe, Argyll
Glenesk Folk Museum, Brechin, Angus
Great Glen Exhibition, Fort Augustus, Inverness-shire
Kilmuir Croft Museum, Portree, Isle of Skye
Lewis Black House, Arnol, Stornoway, Isle of Lewis
Scottish Fisheries Museum, Anstruther, Fife
Shawbost Museum, Stornoway, Isle of Lewis
Skye Water Mill and Black House, Dunvegan, Isle of Skye
Stewartry Museum, Kirkcudbright
Tankerness House, Kirkwall, Orkney
Weaver's Cottage, Kilbarchan, Renfrewshire
West Highland Museum, Fort William, Argyll
The National Museum of Antiquities of Scotland, Edinburgh

Bibliography

Alcock, L., 1972. *By South Cadbury is that Camelot . . .*, London.
Anderson, A. O., 1922. *Early Sources of Scottish History*, Edinburgh.
Boswell, J., 1941. *The Journal of a Tour to the Hebrides with Dr Samuel Johnson*, London.
Campbell, J. F., 1860. *Popular Tales of the West Highlands*, vols I and II, Edinburgh.
  1862, *Popular Tales of the West Highlands*, vols III and IV, Edinburgh.
Campbell, J. G. 1902. *Witchcraft and Second Sight in the Highlands and Islands of Scotland*, Glasgow.
Carmichael, A., 1928, I, *Carmina Gadelica*, Edinburgh.
  1928, II, *Carmina Gadelica*, Edinburgh.
  1940, III, *Carmina Gadelica*, Edinburgh.
  1941, IV, *Carmina Gadelica*, Edinburgh.
  1954, V, *Carmina Gadelica*, Edinburgh.
Collinson, F., 1966. *The Traditional and National Music of Scotland*, London.
  1965. *A History of the Bagpipes*, London.
Cross, T. P. and Slover, C. H., 1969. *Ancient Irish Tales*, Dublin.
Frazer, J. G., 1920. *Spirits of the Corn and of the Wild*, London.
Grant, D., ed., 1956. *The Poetical Works of Charles Churchill*, Oxford.
Grant, I. F., 1959. *The MacLeods, The History of a Clan, 1200-1956*, London.
Graves, R., ed. 1956. *Lucan, Pharsalia*, London, Penguin.
Jackson, K. H., 1940. The Motif of the Threefold Death in the Story of Suibhne Geilt, in J. Ryan, ed., *Essays and Studies presented to Eoin MacNeill*, Dublin.
Jones, G. and T., 1973. *The Mabinogion*, London.
Jones, W. H. S., ed. 1961. Pliny, *Natural History*, London.
Lethbridge, T. C., 1962. *Witches*, London.
Lucan, see Graves, 1956.

MacCulloch, J. A., 1911. *The Religion of the Ancient Celts*, Edinburgh.

MacDonald, Father Allan, *Notebooks*, see Collinson, 1966, 54 fn 3.

MacGregor, A., 1891. *Highland Superstitions*, Inverness.

MacKechnie, J., 1964, ed., *The Dewar Manuscripts*, collected originally in Gaelic by John Dewar, translated into English by Hector M'Lean of Islay, Glasgow.

MacNeill, M., 1962. *The Festival of Lughnasa*, Oxford.

MacPherson, A., 1893. *Glimpses of Church and Social Life in the Highlands of Olden Times*, Edinburgh.

Martin, M., 1934. *A Description of the Western Islands of Scotland*, Stirling, a republication of the original of 1703, London.

Megaw, J. V. S., 1970. *Art of the European Iron Age*, Bath.

Murphy, G., 1953. *Duanaire Finn*, Dublin.

O'Grady, S. H., 1892. *Silva Gadelica*, London.

O'Rahilly, C., 1967. *Táin Bó Cúalnge*, Dublin.

Pennant, T., 1769. *A Tour in Scotland*, Warrington.

Piggott, S., 1962. Heads and Hoofs, in *Antiquity*, 36, 110-18.

Pliny the Elder, see Jones, W. H. S., 1961.

Prebble, J., 1961. *Culloden*, London (1967, Penguin).
1963. *The Highland Clearances*, London (1969, Penguin).

R.C.A.H.M.S., 1974. The Royal Commission on the Ancient and Historical Monuments of Scotland, *Inventory of Argyll, III, Lorn*, H.M.S.O.

Ross, A., 1967. *Pagan Celtic Britain*, London (1974, Cardinal).
1986. *The Pagan Celts*, London.

Shaw, L., 1775. *History of the Province of Moray*, Edinburgh.

Shaw, M. F., 1955. *Folksong and Folklore of South Uist*, London.

Thomson, D. S., 1952. *The Gaelic Sources of MacPherson's Ossian*, London.

Tierney, J. J., 1960. The Celtic Ethnography of Posidonius, in *Proc. Royal Irish Academy*, 60.

Glossary of Gaelic Words

a 'deilbh buidseachd, framing spells, 70
àiridhean, shielings, 136
A 'Mhaighdean, the last sheaf, the corn dolly made from this, 142
bàs, death, 110
bean tuirim, mourning woman, 110
bearradh eòin is amadain air, a punishment by shaving off hair and beard, 145
Benshi, the Fairies Wife, 109
bhàsaich e, he has died, refers to animal, not human, 110
Bliadhna Ur, New Year, 118
Bonnach Brìde, a cake baked on the first day of Spring, 128
Brìde or *Brìdeag*, Little Bride or Brigit, a corn dolly, 127
Brosnachaidh Catha, incentive to battle, 26
bùrn, water, 97
Cailleach, Hag, here the corn dolly made in Glen Lyon from the last sheaf of a bad harvest, 144
Cailleach an Dùdain, The Hag of the Mill-dust, a dance, 150
caisean a 'bhuilg, hide of the bag, the Hogmanay hide, 121
caisean Calluig, the Hogmanay hide, 121
càise Calluinn, Christmas cheese, 123
caisean-uchd, neck or breast skin of beast's hide, 120
caoineadh, keening, 115
Cath nan Coileach, the Battle of the Cocks, a dance, 151
cèilidh, a convivial gathering, 60
chaochail e, he changed, meaning he died, 110
claddach, shore, 97
clann, children, hence 'clan', 23
Clou-an-Beltain, sticks used in Beltain rituals, 135
coronach, lament, 108
corp creadha, clay image, 71
corrach, left-handed, 99
creag, rock, 97
crioslachan, little girdle, 148
Crist, Cristean, the Little Christ, the Baby Jesus, 118
cruaidh, hard, 97
cuach, small round wooden dish, 74
cuid-oidhche, a night's share or portion, 25
Dalta Bride, St Brigit's Foster-Son (Christ), 127
Dagda (Deagh Dia), the Irish God The Good God, 126
Dà-Shealladh, the Two Sights (Second Sight), 55
Dealbh Brìde, St Bride's Image, a sheaf of oats, 128
deirc. alms-giving, 55
deiseal, sunwise

Diardaoin Chaluim-Chille, St Columba's Day, 132
Di- Dòmhnuich-càisg, Easter, 133
Dòmhnach Curran, Carrot Sunday, the Sunday before St Michael's Day, 148
dreug, shooting star, meteor, 114
Droch Shùil, The Evil Eye, 77
Duan Challuinn, Hogmanay poem, 121
Earrach, Spring, 118
eòlas, knowledge, 79
fàidh, prophet, 52
fàireagan na h-achlais, healing of *mam*, q.v., 103
Féis Bride, Bride's (St Brigit's) Feast, 128
filed, seer, 34
Foghara, Harvest, 118
fraoch, war-cry, 25
frith, augury, 49
frithir, augurer, 49
gaire, sour, 97
Geamhradh, Winter, 118
gearradh-chluasach, plant grown from lambs' ears, 134
geasa, tabus, 93
gillean Callaig, Hogmanay lads, 121
gillean Nollaig, Christmas lads, guisers, 118
Gobhar Bhacach, Lame Goat, local name for Last Sheaf, 144
goisearan, guisers, 118
gort, sour, 97
gul or *gal*, professional mourning, 115
Imbolc, Calendar Festival on 1 February, 126
Iolach Mhoire Mhàthair, the paean of Mary Mother, 141
Iolach Mìcheil, Song of Michael the Victorious, 149
Là Beltain, May Day, 134
Là Cath Choileach, The Day of Cock-fighting, St Bride's Day, 129
Là Challiunn, New Year's Day, 119
Là Féill Bharr, Feast of St Barr, 145
Là Féill Bhrìde, St Bride's (Brigit's) Feast Day, 126
Là Féill Moire, Feast of St Mary, 15 August, 140
Latha na Bliadhn' Ur, New Year's Day, 125
laomacha, slice of the caise Calluin, the Christmas cheese, 123
leac struan, a stone used during the baking of the *struan*, 149
Lughnasa, feast in honour of Lugh's birth, 1 August, 16
màm, swelling of the glands, 103
moilean Moire, a bannock made on St Mary's Day, 141
mothan, pearlwort, 73
muime, foster-mother, 75
Muime Chriosda, Christ's Foster-Mother (St Bride), 127
nasg, relieving oneself of the gift of Second Sight, 55
Nollaig, Christmas, 118
Nollaig do Sprèidh, special attention to livestock at Christmas, 119

Motif Index

These numbers are from Stith Thompson, *Motif-Index of Folk Literature*, 1966.

General Index